I0803795

GHOSTS OF THE TRIAD

GHOSTS OF THE TRIAD

TALES FROM THE HAUNTED HEART OF THE PIEDMONT

MICHAEL RENEGAR + AMY SPEASE

Haunted America

Published by Haunted America
A Division of The History Press
Charleston, SC 29403
www.historypress.net

Copyright © 2011 by Michael Renegar and Amy Spease
All rights reserved

Front cover: Korner's Folly. *Courtesy of Camel City Spirit Seekers.*
Back cover: *Photo by Amy Spease.*

First published 2011

Manufactured in the United States

ISBN 978.1.60949.140.6

Library of Congress Cataloging-in-Publication Data
Renegar, Michael F., 1969-
Ghosts of the triad tales from the haunted heart of the Piedmont / Michael Renegar and Amy Spease.
p. cm.
Includes bibliographical references (p.).
ISBN 978-1-60949-140-6
1. Haunted places--North Carolina--Piedmont Triad Region. 2. Ghosts--North Carolina--Piedmont Triad Region. I. Spease, Amy. II. Title.
BF1472.U6R455 2011
133.109756'6--dc23
2011024495

Notice: The information in this book is true and complete to the best of our knowledge. It is offered without guarantee on the part of the author or The History Press. The author and The History Press disclaim all liability in connection with the use of this book.
All rights reserved. No part of this book may be reproduced or transmitted in any form whatsoever without prior written permission from the publisher except in the case of brief quotations embodied in critical articles and reviews.

Michael would like to dedicate this work to his parents, Flay and Katie Renegar.

Amy would like to dedicate this work to her loving husband, David, her children, Rocky and Jade, and her Pawpaw Nelson.

We both would like to dedicate this book to Professor Alvin Proffit and the late Frances Casstevens.

CONTENTS

Acknowledgements

Michael and Amy would like to thank our parents, Flay and Katie Renegar and Michael and Angie Messick, and Amy's Pawpaw Nelson. Amy sends a special thank-you up to heaven to her grandmother, Mary, and Michael to all his grandparents, John and Viola, George and Ruby Caroline, Shober and Victoria and Charles and Nancy, and his great-aunt, Nat Canter. We know they are all looking down on us and are proud of our accomplishments. We'd also like to thank Amy's husband, David, and her kids, Rocky and Jade. We appreciate your patience and assistance while we were putting this book together.

We'd also like to thank Jessica Berzon at The History Press for her belief in this project and for giving us the time to get it together, as well as for countless questions we had to ask. Thanks to Hilary McCullough for her work in editing. And thanks to The History Press itself for showing an interest in our little area of North Carolina and its haunted heritage.

Thanks to David and Anne and Kristen and Ann for taking part in Camel City Spirit Seekers and helping out with info and support. Thanks also to Bo, Jay, Tiffany, Ray and Angela from Mystery Inc. for their assistance on investigations and for providing information on their trip to J.H. Adams Inn. Thanks to Professor Al Proffit of Appalachian State University, a veteran ghost investigator, mentor and friend.

Thanks to Karen and Larry at the High Point Public Library for helping with tracking down leads on the Spookwoods story, as well as on the J.H. Adams Inn. Thanks to Sarah, Michelle and Steve for the tour of the Kersey

Valley site; to Mr. Leigh Davis of the Davis Funeral Services in High Point for sharing information on J.H. Adams Inn; and to Mr. John Trojanowsky, who provided valuable information on Aycock Auditorium and UNCG.

We would like to send regards to Becky Allison and Carolyn Haigwood, who were once an integral part of our group, and to Jamie Dietz, Elissa Gall, Tiffany and everyone who provided intel on the ghostly goings-on at Salem College and Academy, Greensboro College, etc. Thanks to Deonna Kelli Sayed of Haunted NC and Bruce Frankel at Korner's Folly. Without those of you who shared your experiences, we could not have made this book a reality. If we have left anyone out, please accept our humble apologies and our sincere thanks!

INTRODUCTION

We are ghost hunters. How is *that* for an icebreaker? Often, the first question we hear is, "Do you really believe in ghosts?" I always bite off the sarcastic response that tries its best to cross my lips and reply, "Of course."

Our group, Camel City Spirit Seekers (CCSI), was created in 2009 as a successor to Project Ghost-Find. We are based in Winston-Salem but look into ghostly legends all around. Our main area of investigation is the Piedmont of North Carolina. The Piedmont stretches from the foothills of Wilkes County, east to around Raleigh, and from Mount Airy in the north to Charlotte in the south. The Piedmont, whose name refers to the area at the foot of a major mountain range, draws its name from the old European kingdom of Sardinia-Piedmont, which was situated at the foot of the Alps. The Blue Ridge Mountains of the Appalachian Range overlook the western reaches of our Piedmont.

The Triad is the beating heart of the Piedmont. This sub-region is formed by a triangle of cities in Forsyth and Guilford Counties. The western point of the Triad is the twin city of Winston-Salem, home of R.J. Reynolds Tobacco Company, historic Old Salem and Wake Forest University. From here, the northern side of the triangle proceeds east through Walkertown and Kernersville to the eastern point, the city of Greensboro. This large city is named for General Nathanael Greene, a hero of the American Revolution. It is home to Piedmont-Triad International Airport, Guilford Courthouse National Battlefield, and several colleges and universities. The

Do you see the anomaly? *Photo by Michael Renegar.*

eastern side of the triangle draws southwest through Jamestown to the city of High Point, home to one of the largest annual furniture markets in the country. The western side of the triangle goes northwest to Winston-Salem, cutting through the extreme northeastern corner of Davidson County.

The Triad is steeped in the history of our state and, indeed, our nation. During the American Revolution, British general Lord Cornwallis pursued General Greene through the area, fighting several skirmishes and a major battle. Though left largely intact, the region did see several skirmishes during Stoneman's Raid and the failed march of Sherman's Corps as they tried to unite with Grant's forces in the latter part of the War for Southern Independence. In the late nineteenth and early twentieth centuries, several giants of industry made their fortunes in the Triad, including R.J. Reynolds, the Hanes Brothers, Moses Cone and the Davises of Davis Department Stores.

Even earlier, the Moravians, a conservative German Christian sect, settled the area around Winston-Salem, called the Wachovia Tract. They built three settlements: Bethania, Bethabra and Salem. Their mark and influence is still

The authors at Spookywoods. *Photo by Sarah Sherman.*

felt in the area, most directly in the historic community called Old Salem, a living history museum complex.

It should be no surprise that, as the region has been occupied since before our nation was born, including by the Cherokee and Saura Indians, the Piedmont is rich in tales of ghosts and other supernatural creatures. The Triad itself is home to many compelling legends. In this tight little area, we have such long-standing legends as the Little Red Man, the immortal Lydia of the Underpass, a famous vanishing hitchhiker and spectral ghosts of soldiers from both sides of two wars. Also in our Triad, you will find the sad ghosts of children, grey spinsters and college students, as well as animals and even a dark entity or two.

So join us on a tour of the Triad's haunted places. We will tell you the stories of the dearly departed—or perhaps they haven't departed at all!

THE GHOSTS OF OLD SALEM

Old Salem is one of the oldest settlements in Western North Carolina. It was initiated by the Germanic Christian sect called the Moravians, and the first settlers arrived from nearby Bethabra in 1766. It was once a separate town but merged with its neighbor, Winston, in 1913 to form the new city of Winston-Salem. Today, it has been re-imagined as a series of living history museums, complete with costumed docents and private homes and businesses operated in accordance with rules that maintain the spirit of the old town.

There are also *other* spirits present, according to various legends. One of the earliest and most famous of these is the Little Red Man. In life, he was known as Mr. Andreas Kremser. The moniker comes from a very distinctive red coat the well-known man, a cobbler by trade, usually wore.

Kremser lived with other single men in the Single Brothers' House. One evening in 1786, while working in the basement of the house digging out to expand the cellar, Kremser was buried alive by shifting earth. Miraculously, thc poor man was still alive when the other brothers dug him out. He was mortally wounded, however, and though doctors were summoned, they could do little for the broken man. He lingered into the night but died in the wee hours of the next morning. The cobbler was laid to rest in God's Acre, the portion of the community cemetery reserved for members of the Moravian Church.

Thus the story of Andreas Kremser ended…or did it? From the time of his death until well into the twentieth century, Andreas was said to still be

The Single Brothers' House. *Photo by Michael Renegar.*

around. People heard strange noises, much like a shoemaker's hammer, at all hours of the day. From the corners of their eyes, people would glimpse a short human form and a flash of red, said to be Kremser's well-known red coat. Any unexplained occurrence was attributed to the restless specter now called the Little Red Man.

The ghost was reported to be playful. Several children reported encounters with an odd little man who would talk to them or play with them. He could also be a bit mischievous. Once, two men were discussing the ghost in the cellar of the Single Brothers' House when Andreas suddenly appeared right in front of them. The men tried to grab him, but Kremser vanished immediately. He reappeared across the room, brazenly waved his fingers at them and, with a huge smile, disappeared again.

Early in the twentieth century, a visiting minister was talking with a local clergyman. Inevitably, the subject of Andreas Kremser's active ghost came up. The visitor decided that the ghost, though apparently harmless, should be exorcised. With this rite performed, the tenure of Andreas Kremser at Old Salem came to an end. But to this day, any odd noise or strange occurrence is blamed on the Little Red Man.

Another legend centers on the ancient Salem Tavern. The original tavern was built in 1771 and was one of the first public buildings in town. It was widely known for exceptional hospitality and wonderful food. The first tavern was destroyed by fire in 1784, but it was rebuilt within the year.

Through the years, many famous and illustrious people patronized Salem Tavern—scholars, statesmen, generals, many founding fathers. George Washington himself arrived for a stay in May 1791. The building was host to many happy travelers over the years but also saw its share of tragic events.

During the Revolution, a soldier named William Brown became ill due to an injury. He was unable to travel, so his unit moved on, leaving him in the care of the operators of the tavern. Brown eventually developed gangrene. The stench became overwhelming for the guests and workers, so the wretched man was moved to the tavern's smokehouse.

Brown died in agony in the smokehouse on August 17, 1780. Moravian records indicate that the poor man's body had begun to rot and be eaten up with worms while he yet lived. He was buried in the Strangers' Cemetery, which was set aside for those of the community who were not members of the Moravian Church. But for many years, his ghost was said to haunt the place where he had died. Disembodied footsteps, loud moaning and a dark shadow were attributed to the fallen soldier. His ghost was also said to manifest in an overwhelming, foul, intolerable odor.

Salem Tavern's most famous ghost story, however, seems to arise from the death of a tavern guest on September 6, 1831. A man named Samuel McClary had traveled to Virginia's Mineral Springs seeking a cure for an undisclosed illness, perhaps smallpox. Whatever the illness, the cure did not succeed. His health failing, McClary began the long journey home. At the end of August or early September, the coach carrying Mr. McClary arrived at Salem Tavern.

The man was desperately ill. He stumbled into the tavern and collapsed heavily on the floor. The tavern keeper sent one of his slaves for a doctor and helped another to carry the man up to a room. When the doctor arrived, he realized the man was deathly sick. He could do nothing to save McClary, who lapsed into a coma and died before dawn.

The man had never spoken, and no one knew his name. The coach driver had left the sick man's things and moved on along his route. The keeper searched his belongings, hoping to find something to identify him. He found nothing, however, so the Moravian Church took charge and buried the mysterious traveler in the Strangers' Cemetery. The man's belongings were placed in storage.

Shortly after the stranger's death, unsettling things began to occur in Salem Tavern. The slaves and employees began to whisper that "something" was haunting the tavern and its grounds. Unexplained noises, creepy, echoing footsteps and strange moving shadows were noticed by several people. The tavern keeper tried to laugh it off, but the servants continued to be afraid. Finally, one night, one of the female servants burst into his office and shrieked, "Something awful is in the hall!"

The keeper was quite annoyed. Leaving the trembling young woman in fear, he walked out into the dimly lit hallway. In the flickering candlelight, he didn't notice anything at first—but then he saw it. The keeper's heart was filled with horror and dread. A shadowy apparition loomed before him! The tavern keeper recognized the clothes as those his guest had been buried in. He almost turned to run back to his office and slam the door, but something made him stop. The ghost, which had no face, was reaching out to him beseechingly. In a raspy voice, it cried, "Help me!"

The keeper's heart skipped. He stuttered, "Wh-what can I do?"

Salem Tavern. *Photo by Michael Renegar.*

"My name is Samuel McClary," the spectral form replied. "I am begging you…Please write to my brother in Texas and tell him I have passed away. My family is terribly worried over my fate!"

Touched, despite his fear, the keeper promised, "I will do what I can!"

The ghost thanked him, gave him the address and name and then vanished before the frightened keeper's eyes. Shaken, the keeper returned to his office, shooed the terrified maid away and sat down to pen the letter. He posted it the very next day.

Several weeks passed with no new appearances by the ghostly visitor. Then, two new strangers appeared in town. They were Samuel McClary's brother and sister. The pair had come to retrieve their brother's belongings and, possibly, his remains. Though they were given his things, it isn't clear whether the Texan was disinterred and taken home. His purpose achieved, the ghost of Samuel McClary never again disturbed the workers and guests of Salem Tavern.

The ghostly legends of Salem Tavern continued though. Along with the poor soldier, stories have persisted of a ghostly face being seen in a window of an upper floor. This is said to be the specter of one William H. Lutterloh, who suffered from dementia and either fell or leaped to his death from the window.

Then there is Augustus Staub, a German immigrant who arrived in Salem in 1847. He had a fascination with chemistry that would prove fatal. On the night of August 2, 1857, there was a tremendous explosion at Salem Tavern (by that time called Salem Hotel). The smell of volatile chemicals hung in the air. Apparently Staub, ever the amateur chemist, had mixed the wrong ingredients and BOOM! A member of the Moravian Church, Staub was laid to rest in God's Acre. The building was heavily damaged. The owner, Adam Butner, sued the dead man's estate and was awarded money for repairs. Staub's ghost is said to haunt the room where he met his untimely end.

Salem Tavern no longer serves guests. It is one of many living history museums in the Old Salem complex. But echoes of the past still linger in the old place, and the Salem Tavern Annex next door is alleged to be haunted. It is home to the Salem Tavern Restaurant. Perhaps Brown, Lutterloh, Staub and company enjoy visiting patrons of that establishment.

From a Darker Place

Waughtown is one of many historic areas in Winston-Salem. The community is rich in history, steeped in the industrial growth of the late 1890s and the early twentieth century. One of the largest and most successful of the businesses that arose in the area was the J.I. Nissen Wagon Works. Established in 1834, by 1870 the complex had spread to cover a six-hundred-acre tract.

The Nissen business flourished into the 1900s, when the rise of the automobile put an end to the use of horse-drawn wagons. Over the years, thousands of men and boys worked, sweated and bled, producing sturdy wagons. There is little wonder that, to this day, echoes of their work can still be heard. Though the wagon works are long gone, replaced by homes and various small businesses, some say the spirits of those long-ago laborers continue going about their routines.

In the early mornings, as people rise for breakfast and shopkeepers prepare to open their stores, the sound of a blacksmith's hammer can be heard, clanging and ringing out, echoing among the homes and businesses along Waughtown Street, Pleasant Street and other streets in the area. One may also hear the neighing of horses and the clop of their hooves. And in the mists of early morning, the indistinct gray forms of men and boys can be glimpsed working on wagons and doing jobs that haven't existed for one hundred years.

In 1986, Amy's mom and stepdad bought a home on Pleasant Street, in the midst of Historic Waughtown District. As a child, Amy always enjoyed

The house on Pleasant Street. *Photo by David Spease.*

hearing stories of history and folk tales. Her granny loved to regale Amy with as many stories as she could find. Amy's granny told her about the old days and other things. She told of a certain Ms. Elliot who built the house on Pleasant Street and lived there until she passed away. She told Amy that the sweet old lady died in the front bedroom—which Amy shared with her sisters, Amanda and Amber!

Amy wasn't frightened at all by these stories. She slept quite peacefully in the room, even though she knew Ms. Elliot was still there. She'd sensed the good-natured spirit many times. Her sisters wanted nothing to do with that. They would barely stay in there.

Amy was always comforted by the shade of the departed woman. She felt Ms. Elliot was watching over her and the others like a guardian angel. The old woman had kept a big old grandfather clock, which was long gone by the time Amy's family moved in. "One of my fondest memories from childhood," Amy says, "was the tick-tock of an old grandfather clock. And it would chime on the hour. I'm still not sure why I heard this clock...there wasn't one in the house...But maybe it was Ms. Elliot, sharing her love in this way."

Amy was witness to other ghostly goings-on there as a child. When she was outside, sometimes she would hear horses nearby, though none were anywhere in the area. And she would sometimes see men and young boys in strange, unfamiliar clothing. It wasn't until her granny told her about the wagon works and ghost stories that Amy realized who they were.

Eventually, the family moved, though they did not sell the home. In July 2002, Amy moved back into the house on Pleasant Street, this time with her husband David and two-year-old son, Rocky. She was six and a half months pregnant at the time with her daughter, Jade.

Amy spent many hours alone in the house. She cleaned, painted and did various small repairs, getting the place ready for the family. She'd had many experiences as a child with Ms. Elliot's ghost, so she wasn't afraid. She simply didn't pay much attention to the various odd noises or randomly misplaced tools or objects. But one evening, something happened that got her direct attention.

Amy was once again alone in the house, painting in the kitchen. As she worked, she began to notice odd shadows moving in her peripheral vision. She tried to ignore them, but they began to become more frequent. She'd see movement out of the corners of her eyes, but when she would turn to look in their direction, the shadowy figures were gone. Hmmm… Amy thought. This didn't feel like Ms. Elliot. Finally, she put down her paintbrush and, hands planted firmly on her hips, growled at thin air: "Look! If you think you are scaring me, you're NOT!" This seemed to calm the activity—for a while.

But the atmosphere of the home was changing. David would also notice the unusual energy of the place and knew something unnatural was going on. Though they could still feel the presence of the ever-watchful Ms. Elliot, there was something else. Even after the arrival of baby Jade in October, the feeling of the house continued to grow heavier and darker. At times, the feeling was downright oppressive. Amy began to wonder if she should have the house cleansed.

At the time, the growing family attended regular church services and had become members of a local congregation. Amy was especially active in the church and decided to go to the assistant pastor to seek guidance and help. Instead of being attentive and helpful, as any clergy should be in such a situation, the assistant pastor laughed at her. He then said that maybe they could get some of the deacons to come by and pray at the home—at their convenience. The minister, charged with listening to his congregation and helping in any way possible, just seemed to be brushing her off. Amy asked for help three more times and waited for someone to help. She guesses she'd still be waiting until this day for them. Finally, after months of her calls for help going unanswered, Amy and her family left the church.

Amy knew she had a deep faith in a Divine Power. After leaving this church, Amy still felt this faith, despite the way she had been treated. Her Native American roots called to her, and she continued on a very spiritual path. She began going to the library, researching reports and theories on paranormal activity.

Amy was becoming increasingly alarmed that her home had become a harbor for some dark, negative force. In March 2006, Amy met her best friend and erstwhile big brother, co-author Michael Renegar. He visited the Spease home a month later and knew instantly that something was amiss. There was something that just felt off about the house, and even with all the lights on, it seemed darker than it should have.

In her reading and studies, Amy had learned many theories about the dark shadow people she'd been seeing. Many of these theories held that the shadow figures were not human in nature. Amy was unnerved and concerned that this dark energy was becoming stronger and worse as time went by. Nothing seemed to make it stop. Amy and David burned white candles, burned sage smudge sticks, sprinkled holy water and even used anointing oil to bless the house. Crosses hung on the walls. Though the activity would lessen at times, nothing seemed to work completely. Things would calm down for days, weeks, even months at a time. But the shadows and heaviness would always return, seemingly stranger and angrier each time.

Amy was at her wits' end. Chaos seemed to reign, and nightmares vexed and plagued the young family. The final straw was a nightmare that left Amy afraid to sleep, fearing death would come to claim them all. In the dream, Amy found herself in a funeral parlor. All their loved ones were standing there in tears, wracked with grief. There were four closed caskets in the room. There were flowers and pictures arranged on each casket—photos of Amy, David, Rocky and Jade. A loud voice told her, "It is time to leave this house!"

Amy awoke in a cold sweat. She believed this to be a warning, perhaps from a guardian angel—perhaps even Ms. Elliot—that they needed to move before something tragic befell them. On March 1, 2010, Amy and her family moved out of the house on Pleasant Street to their new home. Their new house is much brighter and friendlier than the old one, and all are much happier. They have much more peace there, and there has been no sign of the shadow figures or the feelings of darkness and doom.

As for the house on Pleasant Street, Amy's stepdad still owns it. The property has been cleaned up, and the house has been painted, but if you drive by there, you can still feel heaviness radiating from it. The house seems to watch you as you go by—like a spider, waiting patiently for an unfortunate fly.

REYNOLDA

CAROLINA ROYALTY, ENDURING MYSTERIES

"What is that supposed to mean?" a woman's voice asked very softly. Michael almost fell out of his chair. It was faint but clear as a bell. Trouble was, when this had been recorded, Michael and fellow ghost hunter Carolyn had been the only two people in the area—and she had *not* said that! Michael looked at her as he took the earphones out.

"So, you heard it too?" she asked. Michael nodded in response. He had heard EVP before, but those had been captured by others. *This* one had come in response to his question, "Is that you causing that heavy feeling in the air?"

The two had been exploring the wooded path behind Reynolda House, trying to find evidence of ghostly activity and using a digital voice recorder to try and get an EVP (electronic voice phenomenon). This is a process in which paranormal investigators call out questions aloud in hopes of receiving a response from any ghosts or spirits present. The reply is usually not heard by people present at the time but is heard only when the recording is played back. Responses so clear are not the norm. They are usually little more than a murmur or whisper. When the voice is so clear, it is called a Class A EVP. Since no other living person was present, and neither Michael nor Carolyn had spoken those words, it would seem to confirm that at least one spirit, a woman, was present at Reynolda.

Michael was pretty sure he knew who this spirit was, too. Because of a tragic historic event from 1932, he felt that the ghost was none other than

The bungalow Katharine built. *Photo by Michael Renegar.*

one Libby Holman, second wife of tobacco heir Zachary Smith Reynolds. Evidence found later would seem to indicate, however, that he was wrong.

R.J. Reynolds—a name synonymous with tobacco and intimately entwined with the fate of Winston-Salem. The shadow cast by Richard Joshua Reynolds Sr., his family and his company is long and wide. It lingers to this day, more than a century after he left his father's tobacco plantation in Virginia to begin his own ventures. Reynolds was born on July 28, 1850, the second son of a well-known planter in Critz County, Virginia. The family home, called Rock Spring, still stands at the foot of No Business Mountain.

R.J. grew up in the midst of the War Between the States, one of fifteen siblings. His older brother, Abram, served as an officer in the Confederate army. A smallpox outbreak during the war took the lives of several of the Reynolds children. Only Abram, R.J., three other brothers and three sisters survived until adulthood.

After the war, the Reynoldses still held a substantial fortune, due to their father's maneuvering. Abram moved to Bristol, Virginia/Tennessee, an oddity with one side of Main Street in one state and the other side in the other state. There, he built a fortune of his own in real estate and other business ventures. R.J. never doubted that he, too, would make a fortune. In his teens and early twenties, he was already showing signs of the business genius he would display throughout his life.

While R.J. had substantial talents of his own, he also felt he might have a supernatural aide. He inherited a coin from his maternal grandfather, Joshua Cox Sr. It was an ancient Peruvian coin said to bring protection and good luck to its owner, who had to have the name Joshua—the fabled "Joshua Coin." This coin would come to have a mystical hold on R.J. and, later, his oldest son. They would kiss it, rub it on papers and stocks, etc. It was said to have protected both Reynoldses and Coxes in war, business and even love.

The Joshua Coin would become something of a legend in itself. Eventually, a story emerged that it was not of Peruvian origins after all but, rather, was one of the original thirty pieces of silver given to Judas Iscariot as payment for betraying Jesus Christ. This seems farfetched, and the origins are unclear. But it was cherished as a good luck piece, something one would not expect from a coin of that ill repute. If ever it passed out of the possession of a Joshua, its power would be broken.

R.J. had been to the North Carolina town of Salem many times, selling his father's tobacco. Two of his sisters graduated from Salem Female Academy, the Moravian finishing school there. There was a large sellers' market in the town, as well as a new rail line. The young man was certain he could see a bright future in Salem. In 1874, at age twenty-five, R.J. Reynolds left Rock Spring Plantation for good. Flush with $10,000 from his father, his interest in the family business, the young man set out for Salem and to conquer the world!

At first, Reynolds planned to set up his first tobacco factory in Salem itself. He deferred to the power of the Moravian Church and the feelings of his new neighbors, however, and instead opened it on Depot Street in Winston, about a mile away.

R.J. lived upstairs in the factory at first and worked side by side with his employees, producing plug chewing tobacco. The new businessman developed a reputation for honesty and for caring for all his employees. The rest is history. In the next several years, R.J. Reynolds Tobacco Company grew exponentially, eventually producing loose-leaf chew, Prince Albert Smoking Tobacco and, finally, ready-rolled cigarettes. One anecdote tells that R.J. sought advice from doctors at the time about the health effects of cigarettes. Assured by them that they were safe, R.J. proceeded with production. While we do not know if this is true, it does make one wonder how the tobacco giant would have reacted to later findings about smoking. If this story is true, he may well have ended cigarette production and taken his company in a different direction. In any event, the business would become an international corporation with operations around the world and a multimillion-dollar empire.

By 1903, R.J. Reynolds was a very wealthy man and growing wealthier by the day. He employed several of his family members, who moved to Winston and Salem. R.J. built a beautiful, turreted house on Fifth Street, where he lived with his elderly mother until she passed away.

The tobacco prince had tons of money, and his power and influence were growing. Now, he needed someone to share it all with, and perhaps an heir or two to whom he'd leave his legacy. The tycoon began to consider settling down. His cousin, Zachary Taylor Smith of Mount Airy, sent his daughter, Katharine, to work for R.J.

Katharine, twenty-four, had recently graduated from Sullins College in Virginia. She was quite intelligent and independent. She was bound and determined to work for a while before marrying. She was a talented artist and taught painting classes in Mount Airy before going to work for her cousin. R.J. courted his beautiful young cousin for a year and then proposed, despite the fact that she was thirty years his junior. Katharine had grown to love her cousin very much, and she accepted. Marriage between cousins was not unusual at that time. They were wed on February 27, 1905.

The couple embarked on a four-month honeymoon, traveling across Europe. Nine months after they returned to Winston, on April 4, 1906, their first son, Richard Joshua Reynolds Jr., heir to the empire, was born.

The family, along with the company, continued to grow and fill the house on Fifth Street. Mary was born in 1908, and Nancy came along in 1910. At this point, doctors advised against more children due to health concerns about Katharine. She became pregnant again, however, and a second son, Zachary Smith Reynolds, was born in November 1911. Doctors now insisted that this must be the final child. Katharine's heart was weak, and another pregnancy could possibly kill her.

Winston and Salem merged into a single town, now called Winston-Salem, in 1913. The new town grew in tandem with its chief employer, RJR. As his empire grew, so did R.J.'s children. He doted on them and played with them whenever he could.

The house on Fifth Street, an avenue referred to more and more as "Millionaires' Row," was full of Reynoldses. Katharine began to long for a country estate outside the busy and increasingly crowded confines of the city. Her vision was of a self-sustained village, and she began to plan it for a tract on NC Highway 67 northwest of Winston-Salem. The first building to open was Reynolda Presbyterian Church, in 1914.

Reynolda. It is a clever play on the family name. Besides the church, there was to be a sixty-four-room bungalow as the main house, residences for staff and their families, a working farm, grand gardens, a school, tennis courts, a nine-hole golf course and a big outdoor pool for the children. A large lake was also built, and R.J. dubbed it Lake Katharine.

R.J. spared no expense for his beloved wife's project, though it was rather grand for his tastes. Katharine got the best architects and landscapers available. Reynolda was an estate befitting the Reynolds family, which was adored by the people of Winston-Salem as if they were royalty—Carolina royalty.

As it came together, Reynolda took on a magical, mystical feel to it, much like the retreat of the Russian imperial family outside their capital, St. Petersburg, the fabled Tsarskoe Selo. A Carolina "Tsar's Village" for the tobacco tsar!

Material shortages due to the First World War caused construction delays. But by R.J. Jr.'s (the boy was called Dick to differentiate him from his father) birthday in April 1917, the main house was ready to receive the family.

Happiness at their new country estate would prove elusive. R.J. fell ill with a strange stomach ailment that spring. The pain grew steadily worse and left him increasingly weak and sapped of energy. In the fall, the sixty-seven-year-old tycoon traveled to Johns Hopkins Hospital in Maryland to consult the country's best doctors.

The doctors were befuddled. They had no answers for the businessman and his family. R.J. had been a heavy drinker for years, and he chewed and smoked his company's products regularly. The doctors advised Katharine that R.J.'s condition was grave and that she should not discuss business around him, as stress would make things worse.

R.J. somehow knew his time was short. The doctors prescribed pain medication and sent him home for Christmas. Reynolds was terribly sick. He was so weak that he couldn't even climb the steps to the master bedroom. A bed was placed in his study on the first floor, surrounded by many of the patriarch's favorite things.

In February 1918, the tycoon seemed to rally, and his health seemed to improve. He was even able to go on a rabbit hunt with Dick. Recovery was an illusion, however. By spring, the tobacco giant was in Jefferson Hospital in Philadelphia, and it was clear to him the end was near. Katharine took Dick to Philadelphia, leaving the younger children with their nanny and R.J.'s brother Will.

Mother and son stayed with R.J. in the hospital. The old man set about setting his affairs in order, discussing the future of the family and company. He talked with young Dick and tried to explain to him how the business worked.

The doctors could do nothing for R.J. He was released from Jefferson in early July 1918. On July 29, the day after he turned sixty-eight, Richard Joshua Reynolds Sr. passed away in his Reynolda study, surrounded by his loving family.

It seemed impossible that the business giant was gone, but gone he was. The children in particular were devastated. Their father's death left a void in each that was never really filled. The funeral of the great man, held on July 31, 1918, shut down the entire city of Winston-Salem. Thousands lined the streets to pay their respects to the beloved man. He had always been generous to his employees and to the area. He was well known for his philanthropy, spending millions to improve things. The Tar Heel tobacco tsar was laid to rest in Salem Cemetery.

In the wake of R.J.'s death, his brother Will took over day-to-day operations at RJR. The children, especially Dick, seemed lost. Katharine would roam the grounds on foot and on horseback when she couldn't sleep.

Katharine Smith Reynolds was only thirty-eight when R.J. died. It was a given in local society that she would remarry; it was not a matter of if, but when—and who. The lonely widow began to spend a lot of time with the Reynolda School's headmaster, J. Edward Johnston. Katharine fell in love with Johnston, who was thirteen years her junior. Smith and the girls tried to be supportive of their mother, but Dick was upset. He viewed it as something of a betrayal of his father, coming so soon after his passing. And therein lies the beginning of a series of tragedies that would befall the Reynolds clan.

In July 1921, Katharine announced her engagement to Johnston. An infuriated Dick flatly refused to attend the wedding. His uncle Will, who also didn't approve of the match, stayed away as well.

The couple went on their honeymoon and then moved into Reynolda upon their return. They promptly sent the recalcitrant Dick off to boarding school. Katharine would visit him, trying to keep peace, and Dick did try to be understanding for her sake, but the relationship remained strained.

The Johnstons began their new life as a couple, traveling to the North often. Many times, the three younger children were left at Reynolda in the care of their nanny, Ms. Van den Berg. They felt increasingly isolated from their mother. In 1922, despite doctors' warnings, Katharine became pregnant. She and Johnston took the younger children with them to New York. Dick was angry but also deeply worried. He knew what the doctors had said after Zachary (called Smith) was born.

On May 1, 1922, Katharine gave birth to a baby girl. The child, who was premature, died quite soon thereafter. Again, Katharine was warned that she must not become pregnant again. Dick confronted Johnston, who protested that it was Katharine who had insisted on having a child.

Katharine and Ed ignored the warnings, and by February 1924, she was again pregnant. Dick, now seventeen, was beside himself with worry. Despite everything, he deeply loved his mother, and he began to harbor thoughts that Johnston was intentionally trying to get rid of Katharine. He argued with Ed again, and Johnston once more said that she had insisted.

The family had returned to Katharine's beloved Reynolda, but this pregnancy proved very difficult. Ed and Katharine left the kids and returned to New York. She moved into Harbor Hospital in March. On May 21, 1924, Katharine gave birth to a healthy baby boy, dubbed J. Edward Johnston Jr. Katharine was overjoyed. But time had run out. On May 24, while still in recovery at Harbor Hospital, Katharine suffered a catastrophic brain embolism. She died instantly. The tobacco tsarina was only forty-four.

The Reynolds children, ages eighteen to twelve, were now orphans. A grief-stricken Dick punched Ed Johnston in the face when he saw him. Will Reynolds and Johnston were named their legal guardians. Eventually, Johnston was replaced by Reynolds cousin Ed Lassiter. Though these men tried to offer comfort and support, the four Reynolds kids were left essentially without direct adult supervision.

Dick drowned his sorrows in alcohol, the air and the sea. He formed several different companies and got heavily into airplanes and flying. But he also became an avid sailor, spending months at a time on his boats. Liquor and depression consumed him, and by 1932, he had done a stint in a British prison for killing a man while driving drunk. After this, he was constantly at sea. Smith idolized his brother. He became an aviator. He would never be the sailor Dick was, but he excelled as a flyer.

These were the early days of aviation, filled with legends like Wiley Post, Howard Hughes, Amelia Earhart and Charles Lindbergh. Smith knew them all and hobnobbed with them. He made quite a name for himself, falling just short of a round-the-world flight when his plane broke down in China.

By the age of twenty, Smith had married, had a daughter and been divorced. In early 1932, he married for a second time, this time to torch singer Libby Holman. This second marriage would prove to be the young heir's undoing.

On the night of July 5, 1932, Smith and Libby hosted a birthday party at Reynolda for Charlie Hill, an aviator friend of Smith's. The party was held at the boathouse on Lake Katharine, down the hill from the main house. The servants marched back and forth, up and down the hill, carrying trays of food and bootleg liquor and beer. This was the height of Prohibition, but the rich had no trouble obtaining alcohol. Moonshine whiskey was readily available on the black market and from 'shiners in the hills and hollows of Yadkin and Wilkes Counties.

Libby became quite inebriated. She began openly flirting with Smith's best friend, Ab Walker. Smith seethed until he could take no more, and an argument exploded between Libby and him. Libby stomped off to the bungalow. Smith lingered a while and then excused himself and went up to the main house as well. Shortly thereafter, the party broke up, and a handful of guests made their way to the bungalow.

Blanche Yurka, a friend of the couple, retired to her room. Babe Collier Vaught, who attended the party with James Shepard, was quite drunk, and she was taken up to another room, where she promptly passed out on the bed. Ab and James remained in the living room. After a while, Smith came downstairs looking for Libby. Neither man had seen her, and Smith returned to the second floor.

A little while later, night watchman W.E. Fulcher was at the back of the house. He saw Libby emerge from the trees, grass stains on her gown at the knees. Ab took her by the arm as she came onto the terrace and led her inside. By this time, Smith had come back down to the living room. When he saw Ab lead the scantily clad, laughing Libby into the house, he turned and went upstairs without a word. Libby noticed his exit. She stiffened, shook Ab off her arm and followed her husband upstairs.

A very loud argument was heard. Ab and James looked at each other. "I think it's time to leave. I'll pick Babe up tomorrow," James said, gathered his coat and left.

According to Ab, a few minutes later, Smith came down the stairs, handed him his wallet and declared, "I am going outside to end it all!"

As Smith went out the door, Ab looked around for a place to set the wallet and ended up stuffing it behind a sofa cushion. He started for the door, but Smith came back in. He glanced at Ab and then went back upstairs without another word.

From this point, the events of that long-ago night become quite murky, shrouded in the mists of time, half truths and outright lies. Almost everything known comes from the testimonials of Ab Walker, Libby Holman and Blanche Yurka. All of these witnesses were often evasive and even changed their stories completely over time. That they never told the complete truth is without question.

Walker claimed he remained downstairs, closing the house up for the night. He said all the servants had been sent home. Around 11:00 p.m., Blanche appeared at the top of the stairs. She called down to Ab that she'd heard arguing. Ab told her it was nothing to worry about, and she returned to her room.

Around midnight, Blanche was startled by a sudden sound. She thought it was a gunshot followed by a scream. She got up and went out to the stairs again. Ab was below. Suddenly, Libby came running down the hall from the master bedroom. She leaned over the rail overlooking the living room, screaming, "Ab! Ab! Smith has shot himself!"

Ab froze for a moment and then raced up the steps and down the hall. Libby, now in a peach-colored negligee, followed. Ab later testified that when he got to the sleeping porch of the master bedroom, he saw Smith lying facedown on the bed and his .32-caliber Mauser semiautomatic pistol on the floor three feet from the bed.

According to Ab, the police were not called immediately due to all the illegal booze lying about. An ambulance was called for, but Ab thought it would take too long, so he, Libby and Blanche bundled Smith into a sheet, carried him down to Libby's green Cadillac and rushed the desperately wounded heir the five miles to Baptist Hospital.

Dr. Alexander Cox was the intern on duty and was the first to minister to Smith. He saw what he believed to be an entrance wound behind the left ear and an exit wound at the right temple. Dr. Fred Hanes was sent for, and Smith was wheeled into the operating room.

At some point, Ab called Ed Lassiter and Reynolds relative J.T. Barnes. Both men rushed to the hospital. When they arrived, they asked if the police had been called. Ab told them he wanted to go back to Reynolda and clear out the illegal booze first; he didn't want trouble for Smith if he survived.

Meanwhile, back at the bungalow, Fulcher and estate manager Stewart Warnken found an annoyed ambulance driver in the driveway. He told them about the report of a person being shot. Concerned, they began a search of the house, which they found to be deserted. They grew more concerned when they found blood on the bed on the sleeping porch and in the bathroom. They did not see a gun anywhere.

J.T. Barnes and Ab arrived and filled the two men in on what had happened. Ab went to shower and change, and Barnes and Warnken went to search for the gun. It was 3:00 a.m. Again, the weapon was nowhere to be found. When Ab emerged from his room, Barnes asked him where the gun was. Ab replied that it was on the sleeping room floor. A third search still turned up no gun.

Back at the hospital, another Reynolds relative, Bob Critz, had arrived. He was sitting with Libby when the doctors emerged with news. There was nothing they could do. Zachary Smith Reynolds had passed away. It was 5:25 a.m. on July 6, 1932.

The police were finally called, and near dawn, around 6:00 a.m., the gun was finally found. It was lying on the sleeping porch, three feet from the bed, in plain sight. Fulcher, Warnken and Barnes all knew it had not been there earlier. Critz, who had come straight to Reynolda, was immediately suspicious. He looked at Ab Walker. "I do not believe you are telling all you know!" he accused. "Why did she do it?"

Caught off guard, Ab Walker shook his head. "That is something I shall take to my grave," he replied. Later, Ab would deny ever saying this.

Law enforcement arrived, and the investigation began. High Sheriff Transou Scott asked Ab why Smith would shoot himself. Ab's choked reply was, "He just thought too much of that…woman!"

Word began to spread that something had happened at Reynolda. The media began to gather. Mary and Nancy, both living out of state, were notified and headed for Winston-Salem. RJR president Will Reynolds, in Kentucky for horse races, rushed home. Dick was off the coast of Africa when word came, and he began a journey home immediately. A trip worthy of Indiana Jones took him a month.

At first, it all seemed pretty straightforward. The sisters, knowing how volatile Smith was, accepted that he had killed himself. Will, however, didn't think so, and Dick flatly refused to believe it. He vowed to pursue the truth and see those responsible punished. The news of Smith Reynolds's death caused a sensation. Fresh from the case of the kidnapping of the Lindbergh baby, reporters now descended on Winston-Salem. Somehow, they seemed to sense that there was more to the story.

There were just too many questions. On July 9, the cause of death was changed from suicide to show that Smith died at the hands of "a person or persons unknown." The same day, Reynolds was buried at Salem beside his beloved parents.

At a coroner's inquest, Dr. Fred Hanes testified that the bullet entered Smith's head at the right temple, traversed the brain at a downward angle and exited behind the left ear. This contradicted the observations of Dr. Cox, but the younger doctor did not publicly contradict the revered Hanes. If it had been known, this discrepancy itself could have ignited the smoldering media. Smith was left-handed and was always seen to fire his pistol with that hand. Why would he suddenly switch hands to kill himself?

Damning evidence soon emerged concerning Ab and Libby. Not only were they changing details in their accounts, but several hospital employees reported catching the two in compromising positions even as Smith lay dying in surgery. One even reported seeing them entwined, half naked, on the floor of an unoccupied room they had provided for Libby.

For another thing, head wounds bleed profusely, yet there was relatively little blood on the sheet on which they brought Smith in. There simply wasn't enough blood on his clothes or the sheet to fit the accounts provided by the two. The doctors and nurses seemed to think he'd been lying there bleeding for some time before he was moved and that bleeding had nearly stopped by the time they brought him in.

Blood at the scene didn't seem to fit either. It was as if the sleeping porch had been cleaned before police could investigate. Though some blood was evident on the sleeping porch and the bed, it was also found in the bathroom: in the sink, on the floor and even on the back of the door. Something just wasn't right. Had they cleaned up the scene *before* taking Smith to the hospital?

Prosecutor Carlysle Higgins decided to pursue charges against Ab Walker and Libby Holman in the death of Z. Smith Reynolds. Initially, the two were charged with murder, but the charges ended up being reduced to manslaughter. The original indictments were handed down on August 4, 1932.

Meanwhile, Dick had arrived in Winston-Salem, and he was on the warpath. He made what he thought had happened clear, and publicly. He intended to see justice done for his little brother. On August 27, in the dead of night, Smith's body was secretly exhumed, and a new autopsy was performed. The results were a potential bombshell. Had they been made public in 1932, even though the evidence was all circumstantial, Ab and Libby would surely have been convicted and sent to prison. The secret autopsy showed that the fatal shot had not been fired from point-blank range right against the head. In fact, it had been fired from three to five feet away. This appears to indicate that the weapon could not possibly have been in Smith's hand when it discharged.

The new autopsy proved moot, however. That fall, just as the trial date neared, Dick and the family did a 180-degree turn. They decided it would be in everyone's best interest if the charges were dropped. They proclaimed that Smith's death was possibly the result of a tragic accident, remaining adamant that he had not intentionally killed himself. The bewildered Higgins complied, and Ab and Libby went free.

Why the sudden turnabout? With the new autopsy report, it seemed clear someone else had held the gun when it fired. A former Reynolda employee told his grandson Bo what he'd seen and heard back then. According to this man, who worked for the Reynolds family for years and knew them well, the family became aware that Libby was pregnant. Though there would be questions about paternity among them, they did not wish a possible Reynolds heir to be born in prison. Furthermore, Libby had made threats of revealing things to the public concerning Smith and the family if the trial proceeded. She intended to air dirty laundry in her defense, not caring about any scandal or how such information might hurt the family or damage her late husband's reputation.

We have no way of knowing what she might have revealed. We believe it is likely she was just blowing smoke, gambling that she could bluff them. In any event, Smith's family were determined that his good name not be dragged through the mud. This, coupled with the child she swore was Smith's, led them to show mercy she didn't deserve, and the prosecution of the case was quashed.

To this day, the truth about the events of that summer night in 1932 is shrouded in mystery. All of the principals involved are long dead. Theories abound, but the truth is, we will never know who actually pulled the trigger and ended Smith's life at age twenty, the very dawn of adulthood.

Within a few years, Dick and Nancy had relinquished their portions of Reynolda to their sister Mary and her husband, Charlie Babcock. The Babcocks made extensive renovations to the bungalow, including a basement play area complete with bowling alley, bar and poolroom and an addition with an indoor heated pool. Their family lived a happy life there, dimming the sadness of the past.

But tragic fate was not done with the Reynolds clan. Mary Reynolds Babcock continued the tradition of giving and was a well-known philanthropist, doing worlds of good for Winston-Salem and the whole area. But like her mother, she was struck down in her prime. She died from cancer in 1954 at age forty-six.

Dick struggled with his demons all his life. After three failed marriages, which produced six sons, he seemed to abdicate all cares and responsibilities and moved to Switzerland. Some of his sons visited him there. They brought to him the Joshua Coin, which their mother—his first wife, Blitz—had kept from him. He was horrified to find that she'd had a hole cut in it and a gem installed. He must have realized that its fabled powers, if ever it had any, were broken forever.

The ailing man broke ties to his children shortly thereafter. He married a fourth time, to a German woman named Annemarie. Dick had been in declining health for years. On December 14, 1964, Richard Joshua Reynolds Jr. suddenly died. The cause was listed as too much oxygen to the brain. He was fifty-eight.

Ironically, Dick's death is as shrouded in mystery as Smith's had been thirty-two years before. He had not seen anyone in months, and right before he died, the sick man rewrote his will, disowning his sons and leaving everything to his new wife. Rumors flew. Some questioned whether Dick had actually married Annemarie or changed the will. The fire was fueled further when it was discovered that the official who married them had not actually seen his face, but only a man's back who signed the papers. And there were no witnesses to the new will (Swiss law did not require one). The family was suspicious that he'd been forced into the marriage and the will changes or that Annemarie might have done away with him already. She made matters worse by at first insisting that Dick be cremated immediately.

The sons raised a ruckus at this and somehow managed to block the cremation. But before they could get there, Annemarie had Dick buried in Switzerland. None of his blood relatives saw his body. They tried to have him exhumed, but Swiss authorities denied that. Dick's body remains interred in Europe, though a monument was placed in Salem Cemetery by Annemarie, due to an uproar in Carolina over his burial overseas. Questions linger to this day, though the Reynoldses were unable to pursue legal avenues due to a settlement reached a few years after Dick's death that did restore some, if not all, of their inheritance.

Tragedy was still not done with the Reynoldses. Of Dick's six sons—Josh, John, Zack, William, Michael and Patrick—Zack took after Dick and Smith in adventurism. He made a name for himself as a pilot and was well known for his cars and motorcycles. Though he continued riding bikes, Zach one day swore off flying because of a premonition. For several years, he did not fly. So everyone was surprised when he agreed to fly in an experimental plane with three young acquaintances.

The four would fly to Devotion, the estate Dick had built in Surry County and where four of his sons were raised. It was such a short flight. What could possibly go wrong? On September 4, 1979, the small plane took off from Z. Smith Reynolds Airport in Winston-Salem, circled around and then headed northwest for Devotion. A short time later, it crashed just off U.S. Highway 52 between King and Pilot Mountain. There were no survivors. Zachary Taylor Reynolds was forty-one.

As for Reynolda, the Babcocks continued to use it as a residence into the '60s. It was eventually donated to Wake Forest University. Today, the bungalow houses a renowned museum of art, and the gardens are a public delight. The other estate buildings now serve as shops and restaurants in Reynolda Village. The outdoor pool has been filled in, and Lake Katharine is slowly being reclaimed by plant life. The boathouse stands silent and empty.

Growing up, we heard stories of ghosts at Reynolda. There was little, if anything, said about the house itself. A few vague anecdotes were passed down of hearing footsteps when no one was there and things like that. More substantial details were available concerning the grounds. Most of the stories we heard were about a mysterious Lady in White who would be seen roaming the gardens, the wooded trails and the shores of the lake. She was most often seen on foot but was seen on horseback a time or two. Witnesses said that a feeling of deep cold often preceded or followed her appearances.

As we said at the beginning, we were sure we knew who this ghostly woman was. We were *certain* it was Libby Holman. Suspicion never left the widow of Z. Smith Reynolds. The rumors were renewed in the '50s, when another husband of Libby lost his life, this time to a drug overdose. But this time she had an ironclad alibi. Libby was out of town when this husband died. The son she named Christopher Reynolds died in a mountain climbing accident at seventeen. Some people thought he looked like Smith; others thought he resembled Ab Walker. Nearly four decades after the Reynolda shooting, in 1971, Libby was found dead in her car inside her garage. It was ruled a suicide though the ignition of the car was turned off. We had always believed she knew more about what really happened than she ever told. Some thought she actually pulled the trigger, whether by accident, in a scuffle or on purpose. We postulated that her tortured spirit may have returned to the place where her life first went so wrong. Turns out that *we* were wrong.

John, a Wake Forest graduate, saw online that we were writing a book and planned to include stories about Reynolda. He contacted Michael. While attending WFU, John and his friends often walked over to Reynolda. At night, they would sometimes gather at the old pool house, where the slide once led to the water. Many times they saw a woman walking around out there, day and night. She never made a sound, and sometimes a strange mist seemed to swirl around her. Even when it was hot out, an unnatural cold seemed to envelop them when the woman appeared. The friends began to joke that she was a ghost. John wasn't so sure that was a joke.

In July 2010, Michael met John and two of his friends, Mark and Todd, at Reynolda Village. They showed Michael where they had seen the woman and gave the circumstances of each sighting. They also indicated then that she wasn't always wearing white. But it was always the same woman.

Michael had several photos of women from the early twentieth century. He separated the three men and showed them the pictures, asking if the ghostly woman was in that group of photos. Each separately identified the same woman as the one they had observed—*Katharine* Reynolds!

Michael was stunned. He'd been so sure they would point out Libby Holman. But upon reflection, he realized it made sense. Katharine put her heart and soul into building Reynolda. She'd spent hours walking about or riding her horses around the estate. And she had found solace in her long nighttime walks after the death of her husband. She is obviously still wandering Reynolda, watching over her beloved creation.

We set out to look into other stories about the estate. Someone told Michael that a black man's body was dumped in one of the ponds in the woods. Michael began asking questions. Ms. Hollingsworth, the personal assistant to Barbara Babcock Milhouse, R.J. and Katharine's granddaughter, told him of an inmate who had fallen through the ice on Lake Katharine. He drowned, and his body wasn't recovered for some time due to currents in the water. Could this be the origin of the story of a dumped body? Some people report an uneasy feeling on the paths around the lake and a feeling of being watched. Could it be the spirit of this unfortunate man?

The haunted pathway. *Photo by Michael Renegar.*

Michael asked Ms. Hollingsworth if there were any stories about the bungalow. She asked Mrs. Milhouse, who said she hadn't heard any. The assistant did tell Michael there was at least one mention of a ghost in an old cabin in Reynolda Gardens. She referred him to a 1966 newspaper article about the gardens. Michael was unable to find any witnesses or details for the cabin, however.

Michael was able to explore the open sections of Reynolda House early one morning in fall 2010. He spent time in the room where R.J. Sr. died and on the famous sleeping porch. There was no indication whatsoever that either room was home to a ghost or even a residual effect. It was quite comfortable, in fact, in both rooms. The only sense he got at all from the sleeping porch was that Smith Reynolds definitely did not have possession of his Mauser when it went off, but he received no indication of who did have it.

The basement was somewhat different. Michael wasn't comfortable down there. He kept feeling that someone else was down there with him, though there was no one to be seen. He kept hearing noises like someone was just around the corner, but no one was ever there. Later, he spoke to Tonya Denny of the Winston-Salem Paranormal Society. She told him that she knew a police officer who once responded to an alarm call at Reynolda. When he got there, there was no sign of anyone, but it sounded as if a party might be going on in the basement. He clearly heard the sound of a bowling ball striking pins. Yet when he went down and checked, there wasn't a soul to be found. He beat as hasty a retreat as possible.

Reynolda is a wonderful place and is open to the public. You may tour the house for an admission fee, and it often hosts events. If you are ever there, listen closely for echoes of the past. And don't be surprised if the woman in period clothes you are talking to simply vanishes before your eyes.

Tales from Salem Academy and College

Salem Academy and College is a highly respected school for women in the heart of Winston-Salem. It was founded by the Moravian Church as Salem Female Academy in 1772. By the mid-1800s, it had become a renowned boarding school famous for its quality education and wonderful environment. By 1866, it was *the* place to send young women for finishing school.

At an institution of such age, with dozens of historic buildings, ghostly legends are almost a given. And indeed, there is a wide array of spooky stories and goings-on reported throughout the campus. Every fall, new students are oriented to the many legends of Salem College.

One of the first stories the girls are told concerns the Clewell residence hall. The story tells of a young girl, between the ages of eight and twelve, who came to visit her sister, who lived in Clewell Hall. At some point, the child began exploring on her own. Somehow, she managed to get inside the elevator shaft and plunged to her death at its bottom. According to legend, the elevator shaft was sealed and never used again.

While it is possible that this accident actually occurred, we could not verify it. As for the shaft never being used again, this is a fact. Actually, there never was an elevator installed, so it was never used to begin with. Some reports indicate that a construction worker was killed when it being built, but this, too, proved undocumented.

Strong Dorm is another building alleged to be haunted. A place called the Friendship Room is said to be particularly active. The spirit that dwells

Salem College. *Photo by David Spease.*

there has a mischievous streak. Among its favorite tricks is to suddenly throw the covers off sleeping students. The ghost will also touch you or brush you gently on the arm.

Gramley Library is another campus haunt. Students claim it is the home of a variety of spirits. In the basement, by the archives, one student told us that a German man seems trapped. He makes his presence known with odd noises, footsteps and a deep, icy cold. The third floor is often the scene of awful, disembodied cries and strange, unexplained lights that flit about. At times, these phenomena have been reported as often as once a week. Supposedly, these haunting incidents are the work of two girls who died in 1907. They were allegedly electrocuted in an accident.

Sisters Hall is one of the oldest buildings on campus. Strange whispers have been reported, and several girls told of being touched inappropriately while in the shower. Kristen Brown always felt uncomfortable in the building. She once felt someone brush by her, seemingly in a hurry. She felt a strange warmth and then an icy cold. Two girls, Elissa and Paula, attempting to record EVP, left a recorder in the stairwell one night. When they played it back the next day, a faint voice said, "Please! Turn on the light, please?"

One of the most talked-about buildings with an alleged haunting is Gramley Dorm, where a student is supposed to have hanged herself on the top floor. Students have often heard the sound of a chair being dragged across the floor and then suddenly knocked over. We met Elissa Gall through Kristen, and she told us several personal experiences in several places on campus, starting with Gramley Dormitory.

Once, Elissa was standing at her mirror when she heard a knock from the other side of the wall. She knocked back and got a response, so she knocked again. This time, the knock was returned, but the sound moved up the wall and across the ceiling. She was quite unnerved by that and even more unnerved when she remembered that the room on the other side of the wall was a locked closet. Elissa was also witness to the sounds of the moving chair overhead. Try as we might, however, we could not find any documentation of the alleged suicide in Gramley Dorm.

Another thing people experience in this dormitory is the sound of marbles hitting the floor and rolling. Yet when anyone goes upstairs to check, the room the noises came from will invariably be empty. And on occasion, girls will hear a knock at their door. When they check, no one is there.

In the room where Elissa heard the knocks, her roommate, Katie, may have come face to face with a full body apparition. One evening while Elissa was studying with a neighbor, Katie was in the room alone. There was a strange sound and then, suddenly, a little blonde girl burst through the door into the room. She was dressed in a Victorian-era dress. The child stopped short when she saw Katie. Just as they made eye contact, the girl turned and ran out the door. Katie was hot on her heels, but the child had vanished into thin air. Katie pounded on the door of the room where Elissa was studying and related, wide-eyed, the incident.

The little girl was apparently known. The girls in Gramley came up with a name for her. They called the child Nancy. They believed her to be the daughter of a Salem minister. Nancy loved to play tricks on the girls and could be really mischievous. Sometimes, she would take small things and hide them. The item would not be returned until the victim of the prank asked Nancy to return it. Many a student searched frantically for something, such as their keys. Only when they would appeal to Nancy was the object found, often right where they'd looked repeatedly.

Babcock Dormitory is another campus building that sees a lot of paranormal activity. The building is named for Mary Reynolds Babcock, daughter of tobacco magnate R.J. Reynolds Sr. A portrait of Mrs. Babcock hangs in the building, and the eyes of the portrait will follow you. Students claim the painting's facial expression changes, too, if you offend her. By tradition, students greet the portrait when they enter and say goodbye as they leave, so as not to disrespect her and bring some sort of paranormal payback on themselves.

Tiffany lived in Babcock with her roommate, Ana. She believes it was in room 121. As Tiffany was moving in and unpacking, she noticed a woman in a white dress with beautiful long brown hair standing in the doorway. Thinking it was a new neighbor, Tiffany turned to greet her. When she spoke to her, however, the woman vanished right before her eyes. Tiffany is a paranormal sensitive, so such things do not bother her. She is used to ghosts, so instead of running, screaming, from the building, she simply shook her head and returned to her task.

About two weeks after classes began, Tiffany was passing by the science building, which has a fishpond in front of it. Tiffany looked up and saw the same woman serenely observing the fish. Again, she disappeared when Tiffany spoke to her. But this was not to be her last appearance.

Just after midterm exams, the girls were exhausted. Sometime around 6:00 a.m., Tiffany awoke suddenly. She could sense a different presence in the room. Ana had also been awakened by something. As Tiffany watched, Ana sat up and looked around. She didn't have her glasses on, but Ana seemed to focus on the middle of the room. "Tiffany?" she asked groggily.

"Yes?" Tiffany responded.

"Is there a woman with long brown hair sitting in that chair?" Ana asked thickly. "And is she wearing a white dress?"

"Uh-huh," Tiffany answered.

"Okay." Ana yawned, rolled over and went back to sleep.

Tiffany remained where she was for while. Finally, as the light grew stronger, the woman faded from view. There was no chair there. Tiffany went back to sleep.

Tiffany began to look into the ghost stories around campus with friends. They recorded several EVP in several campus buildings, including Babcock. Out on Salem Square, they found a huge, ancient tree. Tiffany could feel a sense of death around it. She felt a deep sadness there and got the feeling of a young couple whom she believed may have met their end there. The names Jacob and Elisabeth came to her. The tree is no longer there. We tried to find a couple with those names but were unsuccessful.

Elissa and her friend Paula also did some investigating and EVP recordings. Elissa had gotten really into the ghost stories after her experiences. The old infirmary on campus is often said to be haunted. It is called the Bahnson House, not to be confused with the home of the same name on Fifth Street. Elissa had also lived in this building. Her room was the first room on the left, on the first floor. It had once been a kitchen.

As Elissa sat there one night, the VCR clicked on and off several times by itself. "Please, stop!" Elissa called out, and it did—for a while. But it began to click on and off again and didn't stop this time when she asked. It remained quiet only after the besieged girl got up and unplugged it.

We had heard about ghosts at Salem College many times. So when we decided to do this book, we knew we had to include it. We began our research with relish. It became clear, rather quickly, that we were not going to be able to find documentation of any of the supposed deaths alleged to have caused the hauntings. There were no smoking guns. There was nothing we could find on *any* of them. Neither the worker in the elevator shaft, nor the girl who fell. Not the girl who hanged herself, and nothing on the two supposedly electrocuted. We *were*, however, able to find one historically documented story of a tragic death on campus that might explain the genesis of several of the campus legends. It is the sad tale of Sarah Tilkey.

Sarah, called Salley, was the daughter of John and Malinda Tilkey of Augusta, Georgia. The businessman and his wife had been searching for a boarding school to send young Salley to. They were most impressed with Salem Academy. Salley arrived in Salem in August 1872, when she was fifteen. She was a very bright student and very likeable. She made a lot of friends, and her first year at the school passed happily and uneventfully.

Salley spent the summer of 1873 with her parents and then returned to Salem for the fall term. She began taking piano lessons and studying music theory. Her future seemed to hold exceeding promise.

Friday, November 28, 1873, dawned bright and clear but exceptionally cold. The entire week was unseasonably cold, and the stoves and fireplaces all over campus had been lit. It was bitter cold outside, but the buildings were warm and comfortable. Salley was upstairs, most likely in Sisters Hall, practicing on a piano. An ember from the fire floated over and landed on her dress. At first she didn't notice, but smoke soon began to rise.

Salley tried to put it out but couldn't. She ran into the next room, where some of her friends were. They tried to put it out, but the smoke began to billow more and more. The girl panicked. She took off running down the

Sisters Hall. *Photo by David Spease.*

hall, shrieking for help. This only fueled the smoldering ember, and her dress burst into flames.

"Help me! Help me!" Salley screamed as she ran. "Somebody, *please* help me!"

She must have been a shocking, horrifying sight to anyone who saw her. The dress was fully engulfed as she reached the staircase and began to descend. The poor girl ran down the steps, smoke and flames trailing behind her. Her terrible screams filled the air and echoed through the building.

On the first floor, music professor Edward Lineback heard the awful ruckus. He ran to see what was happening. To his horror, he saw Salley rushing down the steps toward him, completely engulfed in fire. Lineback rushed to grab a blanket to smother the flames. Salley collapsed in a burning heap at the foot of the stairs. Her screaming had stopped. The professor used the blanket to put the fire out, burning his hands seriously in the process.

The fire was out. Lineback covered the horribly injured girl with the blanket, scooped her up and took her to a bed in a nearby room. A crowd was gathering. Girls clung to one another, sobbing. Teachers stood looking about helplessly. Professor Lineback sent for a doctor.

Doctors came, but there was little they could do. It was clear there was no hope. Salley was just too badly injured. Throughout it all, Salley remained calm. Incredibly, she tried to comfort those around her. Every little bit, she would ask about friends and assure her attendants that she had a deep faith and was ready to meet her Creator. Tears fell like rain that day at Salem College.

Salley lingered for several hours. Finally, around 7:00 p.m., she drew her last breath. A pall of sadness settled over the campus. The despairing Professor Lineback sent word to the unfortunate girl's parents.

The Tilkeys arrived on the train from Georgia on November 30, 1873. They were allowed to see Sarah's body. The fire had not touched the child's face. To the grieving parents, she looked peaceful, as if she were just sleeping. They left for Augusta the same day, and Salley was laid to rest in her hometown. That Christmas was one of the saddest Salem College ever saw. This tragic episode was recorded in Moravian Records and in Jennifer Bean Bowers's book *Winston and Salem: Murder, Mystery and Mayhem*.

We have to say that we believe the personal accounts of those who spoke with us. There is something to the incidents they recounted, despite the lack of solid documentation or proof. However, we also believe that certain elements of the sad story of Salley Tilkey have been incorporated into the ghost stories associated with several campus buildings. The accounts of screaming, running footsteps and cold and hot spots all fit.

Whatever their true origins are, the ghosts of Salem Academy and College will continue to go about their business. And their stories will continue to be passed down to new students every fall.

Pawpaw's Message

It was early spring 1984. The time had come to prepare for planting the garden. Aunt Rachel Coleman gathered her tools and other supplies to till the ground and get things going. Little Amy, age three and a half, sat beside the small fishpond playing with her toys. As the little girl sat there, peacefully enjoying her play, a tall older man appeared and sat down beside her.

"Hello, Amy," he said in a kind, gentle tone. "Can I sit here with you while you play?"

Amy smiled. "Yes, Pawpaw, you can sit here with me."

The old man smiled. "Amy," he asked. "How do you know I'm your grandfather?"

"Well, Pawpaw," Amy replied, "you look like my pawpaw in the pictures Nanny Maw has inside. You *are* my Great-Grandpa Elson, aren't you?"

With a big, gleaming smile, he answered her, "Yes! Yes, Amy, I am! But…you can see and hear me. I don't know how you can see and hear me. Do you?"

"No," Amy replied, "I don't know how I can see and hear you. Are you an angel?"

"Well, no, I'm not an angel," he told her. "But from time to time, I do stop in to check on my Dearest Lula and Rachel. I loved all of my family when I was alive. I keep a watchful eye on all my family."

"Even me, Pawpaw?" the wide-eyed child asked.

"Yes, Amy," Elson told her, "I especially watch over you and Pamela. I really wish in life I could have had more time to spend with all my family. I am still here in spirit to watch over the family."

Pawpaw visited Amy several times. *Photo by David Spease.*

"Pawpaw, I wonder why the rest of our family can't see you?"

"Amy, it seems you have a gift that allows you to see beyond death's veil," Elson replied. "I would accept it and be glad of it. Don't be afraid of it because it must be special."

No one is sure why some people can see and speak with the deceased. To this day, Amy has always accepted that it is part of her life, just like Pawpaw Elson told her to.

Amy's Great-Grandpa Elson visited her on many occasions as she grew. He told her stories about her mother and uncle and the family and things they loved to do. As she got older, his visits became more and more infrequent. When he did come, they would talk about gardening and flowers, how to tend the earth and many other subjects. Amy felt touched to receive his wisdom in the old ways of gardening.

One day, while Nanny Maw was fixing lunch, Amy decided to ask about her gift. "Nanny Maw," Amy asked, "have you ever seen Pawpaw Elson since he died?"

Lula paused and then smiled. "Why, yes, Amy, I see him often in my heart and in my dreams." She continued, "He will always be in my heart. I love him and our children with all that I am."

"Well, Nanny Maw," Amy asked, "do you think it is okay to see loved ones or other people who have died?"

Gently, the old woman answered her, "Yes, Amy, I believe it is okay. It could only mean that they want you to see and hear them. And also so you know they can see you. Maybe it is that you could help someone one day even."

As days turned into months and months into years, Amy saw many things. She believed it was a gift from God and was humbled to think that, for some reason unknown to her, she might be able to help the dead, and the living, in some way.

As an adult, Amy has come to better understand death. She believes we should honor our loved ones who have passed beyond the veil. She doesn't believe we need any special powers to communicate with them—no talking boards, pendulums, crystal balls or trance mediums. All you need is love in your heart. They are right there, just on the other side. Though grief can be hard to deal with, one need only believe and say what they mean and feel. Our loved ones are always in our hearts and at our sides in spirit. It may sound silly to some, but it works for Amy and anyone else who truly believes.

A Hanging Sadness

A loud knock sounded on the front door. Amy's next-door neighbor was there. She had been to the store up the street and was returning home when she saw something horrible. When Amy answered her knock, the neighbor gasped, "Amy! The Spanish guy down at the house on the end of Tryon has hanged himself in that big tree in his backyard!"

"What?" Amy cried. "You're serious, aren't you?"

The two women went into Amy's backyard to see if they could see anything. Sure enough, the man's lifeless body hung there in the tree, slowly twisting in the slight breeze. It was clear he was dead, but there was no way to tell how long he had been dangling there. Dread seemed to fill the air with heaviness. The police had arrived on the scene. Amy wondered what on earth could have happened to cause this act of hopelessness.

Later on, Amy remembered something. A friend of hers had rented the house about six years before. One day in the summer of 1995, her friend invited Amy over to the house. With her mom's OK, Amy went on over. Even as she entered through the front door, Amy felt uneasy. She sensed something heavy and a certain sadness. She felt somewhat sick to her stomach. But she forced the feeling aside for her friend's sake. He had been making repairs for the landlord, and Amy was proud of his accomplishments with the house.

Amy hugged her friend Kerry and told him she liked what he had done. He showed her around a bit. As they went into the kitchen, Amy

A hanging sadness. *Photo by David Spease.*

was seized by a deep chill. It surrounded her and filled her, though it was eighty degrees outside. It was as if the past were trying to manifest. Amy's hair stood on end, and she could stay just a few moments more. Without a word to Kerry about the unusual feelings, Amy excused herself and left.

Kerry moved out of the house just a few weeks later. But on that particular day, although the cottage seemed peaceful and quiet, Amy could just feel it. Something just wasn't right with that property. She sat down on the front steps to ponder the house and what was going on there.

Try as she might, Amy just couldn't put her finger on it. Finally, after quite some time, she decided to go home. As the young woman stood, she swooned, her head swimming. She nearly fell to her knees as despair, dread and an infinite sadness washed over her. A deathly cold shot through her body for a few seconds. The sensory overload passed as quickly as it came, and Amy raced back to her own home as fast as her legs would carry her.

As she stood on her own front steps, Amy took several deep breaths. Though the direct feelings had departed, she could still feel residual affects of what she'd just experienced. She had been jolted to her core. As she stood there, she felt cold all over and winded from her mad dash. She became very uncomfortable. It felt like someone—or something—was watching her every move. "Oh me!" she gasped as she went inside and ran to her room. What had just happened? For years afterward, Amy did everything she could to avoid that eerie house.

In 2010, Amy was reminiscing with her mom, Angie, and her uncle Clint. Amy and Angie started talking about the Spanish man who had hanged himself in the backyard of the house on Tryon Street in Winston-Salem. Amy said how odd and sad that was. Clint looked at her with a strange smile. "Well," he said, "I know something else about that old place."

Amy and Angie listened intently as Clint told them what he knew. The house had stood vacant for a decade, but from about 1972 to 1974, the place had been a party pad for local teens. Before, a happy family of three had lived there, in the 1950s or early '60s. One day, the husband and child, a girl, died in a terrible car wreck. A short time later, the despondent mother and wife committed suicide—by hanging herself in the backyard.

Amy was shocked. Suddenly, she remembered the strange feelings she'd experienced. Now it made sense. And how strange that the poor man who lived there later had done the same thing from the same tree. But Clint's revelation was not finished. According to tradition, there was an old rocking chair sitting in the front room of the house. The chair was said to have belonged to the poor lady who killed herself. Locals told that if you moved that chair, it would return to its original position, no matter where you moved it. Clint had seen it rock by itself on occasion. One night, Clint and his friend Jackie were messing around in the abandoned house. They figured the tale of the chair was a load of nonsense. Clint grabbed the chair and hauled it across the room, against the opposite wall. The young men looked around, and only seconds later, they looked to find the chair back in its original spot! The boys scrambled to escape the house, Clint using a window instead of the door.

Amy and Angie were stunned. Amy then remembered someone telling her about the lady who would watch his every move when he was near the house. He was terribly afraid of her—even more so after she died.

No wonder Amy had felt such strange things from the old cottage. Its history was quite grim. Had the despair of the lonely, heartbroken woman lingered, embedding in the very walls of the house? Did the Spanish man become so overwhelmed by the oppressive sadness in the house that he followed in the footsteps of the previous resident? Or is there something else there, forever waiting to claim another victim? Either way, the doleful cottage has claimed two despondent souls. Let's hope that is all—for the house is occupied once again.

Three Little Indians and Other Tales

Amy's mom, Angie Messick, and her brother, Clint, told Amy about growing up in an ancient house, built around 1818. Angie was ten when they moved in, and Clint was about fourteen. They lived with their grandparents, Elson and Lula Coleman, her mother, Mary, and their aunt Rachel in the two-story home.

The house is long gone now but stood between Abbotts Creek Church Road and Curry Road on Old Highway 311 in a rural section of Kernersville known locally as Horneytown. Old-timers in the area call the region Arrowhead Country. The moniker fits, for the fields, especially right after being turned, were full of the Native American artifacts. Flint, marble and quartz could also be found all around. Clint recalls that the area had "one heck of an eeriness to it all."

One afternoon, Angie set out for the woods and fields behind the house. One of the little girl's favorite pastimes was to search for the Indian arrowheads. She spent quite a while scouring the clearings and fields for the artifacts. Finally, she stopped to look over her new arrowheads. Suddenly, as she stood there, she realized she was not alone. She looked up and saw three Native American children, dressed in traditional Indian attire, romping and playing nearby. There were two girls and a boy. They didn't notice her, standing there, watching them play as the day began to drain away. Finally, afraid at what she had seen, Angie took off running for home. She didn't dare look back, lest she see an Indian chasing her. She never went back to that particular field alone again.

Something followed him in the woods beside the road. *Photo by Michael Renegar.*

Clint also experienced odd things out there. He told Amy about one evening when Elson sent him off to the Little Cedar Grocery, about a mile toward Winston-Salem on Old 311. The boy set out on foot as dusk fell. As he walked along, darkness began to creep up on him. Chills ran up and down his spine. As the darkness grew thicker, he began to feel as if he was being watched. Something was in the woods. He picked up his pace. By the time he reached the store, he was running.

"Eerie!" he snorted aloud and then went inside.

Clint came out after a few minutes and started home. It was darker still, but there was still a bit of light from the departed sun and from passing cars. The feeling of being watched returned. And now, he felt he was being followed. In the woods, he occasionally saw dark forms or shadows. Some looked like people—Indians. Others looked like…he knew not what. Someone seemed to be moving along beside him in the woods. Clint stopped. "Hello?" he called out.

There was no answer. He was pretty sure he was glad of that. The shadow figures were moving again. Were they moving closer? Clint took off and ran for home as fast as he could move. He was nearly out of breath when he finally went inside the old house. "Whew!" he gasped. "What the Heck was *that*?"

From then on, Angie and Clint experienced something of the dark presence every time they ventured out. A sense of relief came when they finally moved away.

Just a few miles up 311 is the Union Cross Fire & Rescue Station. For years, local ghost hunters have heard that this building is home to a very active spirit. It has supposedly unnerved even the bravest of men. Contrary to popular belief, however, the phantom has never sent any of the firefighters running screaming from the building.

There are radios and a television set that have been known to turn themselves on and off, even when unplugged. And objects do move of their own volition at times, and people have experienced being touched. The crew people blame the incidents jokingly on Pops. There once was a bar behind the emergency building. Pops ran this bar. One evening, Pops died in his bar. Ever since, ghostly activity has been reported in the vicinity. Maybe Pops is still looking for customers to serve drinks to.

In their book *Triad Hauntings*, Burt Calloway and Jennifer FitzSimmons told the story of a hitchhiker who had a bad encounter with something off Glenn High Road. The events of the story take place near the intersection with Oak Grove Road. The man was walking along Oak Grove, beside the cemetery for Glenn View Baptist Church, which was once called Oak Grove. Something shoved the fellow, but no one was there. Just when he thought he was just imagining it and had stumbled, it happened again. This time, he fell. The fellow jumped up and ran, terrified, until a passing motorist stopped and picked him up. Others have been terrorized by the unseen force here, being touched, pushed and even scratched. Todd S. told me the whole area, especially the church grounds, gives him the creeps.

Calloway and FitzSimmons also related the story of a young man named Skip who was killed in a tragic accident on August 17, 1980. The ghost of the young man returned to his mother's home in Walkertown the day after his funeral. His mom, Shirley, heard his voice telling her not to cry. As time passed, she received other signs that he was still around. Lights would go on and off in the house. They seemed to follow patterns similar to those of Skip when he was alive.

One day, Shirley was sunbathing beside her son's car. Suddenly, the driver's side door opened of its own volition; no one was around it. Another time, the woman was driving with a friend near where Skip died when they saw a pedestrian walking on the side of the road. Both women recognized him as Skip. When they turned and went back, he was gone.

Skip's mother has since passed away, but Skip allegedly remains on the road where he died. Numerous people who knew Skip have seen him standing or walking along the road where a car hit and killed him.

We spoke to a classmate of Skip's from the Glenn High class of 1979. Though *Triad Hauntings* locates the scene of the accident on Highway 158 near Walkertown, where he lived, the fatal accident actually occurred on Sedge Garden Road, about 3/10 of a mile from its intersection with Highway 150, in southern Kernersville. Trooper R.D. Woods reported that Calvin T. "Skip" Westmoreland Jr. was struck by a car there around 3:45 a.m. and was killed instantly. This is several miles from the place described by the authors of *Triad Hauntings*, but this is definitely where Skip died and where his ghost has been seen. This is the first time we have personally been able to find actual documentation for a roadside revenant. We plan to take an excursion to the scene to see if we might contact Skip and perhaps convince him he can move on now and join his beloved mother on the far side of the Jordan.

These are just a few of the tales from the rural heart of the Triad. The area described is in the west-central part of the region, set in the midst of the three cities that form its points. The more we dig, the more we are sure to find.

Korner's Folly

It was a bright sunny day in 1878. Jule Gilmer Korner and the crew he had hired were hard at work on the new house on Main Street in Kernersville. It was to be his home, art studio, office and display area for his interior designs. It would also have a carriage house and stables attached.

The frame soared more than three stories into the air already. One of the neighbors stopped to watch. The floor levels seemed haphazard and off kilter. The farmer shook his head and declared, "Surely this will be Jule Korner's folly!"

The name stuck! Korner liked it so much that he incorporated the name in the sign out front. To this day, the building is known as Korner's Folly.

Jule Korner was born Jule Kerner in 1851. He became famous for his Bull Durham paintings of bulls across the South. Besides being an accomplished artist, he was also an interior designer and decorator. His eclectic home showcased his myriad talents. From the outside, the unique building appears to be a three-story mansion. However, inside, there are *seven* levels from cellar to attic! Fifteen fireplaces, all of different designs, adorn many rooms of the house. But none of them was ever used; Korner was completely terrified of fire from his youth until his death. Twenty-two rooms fill the seven levels, from child-sized nooks to a grand reception room. The ceilings range from six feet to twenty-five feet in height.

Jule Korner's Folly. *Photo by Amy Spease.*

One may be tempted to compare Korner's Folly to the infamous Winchester Mystery House in San Jose, California, but this isn't quite accurate. Sarah Winchester was driven mad by her obsession with the house and the spirits of all the dead who were killed by the rifles created by her husband's family. She actually built the home more for them than herself. The Winchester House has stairs to nowhere, doors that open on walls, rooms within rooms, etc. Jule Korner, however, was quite sane. He built his house with deliberation, intending each room to show something different about his designs. But like the fabled Mrs. Winchester, Korner continued to add to and build on his house until the day he died.

He moved into the grand mansion in 1880. He brought with him a faithful servant, former slave Clara "Aunt Dealy" Korner. Aunt Dealy had practically raised Jule and his older brother Joseph after their mother passed away in 1853. The Korner boys were quite fond of Aunt Dealy, and she remained with them, more family member than slave or servant, until she passed away in August 1896 at seventy-six in the cottage Jule built for her behind the Folly. The beloved woman is buried in the family plot behind Kernersville Moravian Church. Aunt Dealy lived in the main house until 1886, when Jule married Miss Polly Alice Martin. The cottage she moved to now serves as the offices and gift shop for the Korner's Folly Foundation.

Jule and Polly Alice had two children, son Jule G. Korner Jr. and daughter Dore. The children grew up in the eclectic home. In 1924, Jule Korner Sr. passed away at age seventy-four. The workmen's hammers were still pounding the day he drew his last breath. The family continued to live there for many years.

In 1970, Korner's Folly was placed on the National Register of Historic Places. Today, the house is a museum run by a nonprofit organization, the Korner's Folly Foundation. The group is dedicated to restoring the grand dame to its early glory. Central air and heat were installed in 1999–2000.

The museum features paintings by Jule Korner, his cousin Jean Baptiste Kirner from Germany and German master Caesar Milch. Milch actually lived with the Korners and is said to have died in either the main house or in Aunt Dealy's cottage.

We have always thought the Folly *looked* as if it should harbor a ghost or two. In 2009, we began to hear rumors that it was, in fact, haunted. Turns out, there had been stories about ghosts in the old place for decades, but they were kept carefully under wraps for years. A change in management seems to have opened up the doors, so to speak.

In January 2011, Michael called the offices making inquiries as to the possibility of paranormal activity. The next day, Executive Director Bruce Frankel returned his call. The director was very open to the idea of discussing and exploring the ghost stories of Korner's Folly. In fact, several official investigations had already been undertaken. He put us in touch with Deonna Kelli Saayed, the Folly's paranormal advisor, and a member of the group Haunted NC. On January 28, 2011, she met Amy, Michael and Michael's mother, Katie, at the Folly for an interview.

Amy and Katie explored the home while Deonna and Michael sat down in a sunny room by the kitchen to discuss the Folly and its ghosts. Katie came and sat down with Deonna and Michael as they were getting started with the interview. She said she felt a warm and welcoming feeling, not anything scary. Deonna agreed and said that was what most people felt. Amy later also described the spirits she sensed as friendly and welcoming.

As they started the interview, Michael turned on his digital voice recorder to help with notes and also in hope of possibly capturing a ghostly EVP. Deonna told us that most of the paranormal activity recorded in the Folly is aural in nature, though apparitions have been seen on occasion. Most investigators report capturing male and female voices in the building, mostly children. This is not surprising, as there have been many performances of children's theater in the open theater upstairs.

The house shows signs of both intelligent entities and residual activity. Residuals are actually just place memories, like a recording that plays over and over. There is no actual spirit involved, normally, and the "ghosts" do not usually react to people or events around them. Intelligent entities are actual spirits that interact with people and the environment. These will often respond to direct questions.

As they sat talking, Michael noticed that the recorder, with fresh batteries, was indicating low power. He mentioned this, and Deonna said that happened sometimes. A quick drain of fresh batteries can indicate the presence of a spirit in the vicinity. Some theories hold that they draw energy from electronics to manifest. Nothing appeared to them, though, so they continued talking.

Deonna told them about an incident from one of the very first official investigations in 2009. As the group was setting up cameras, video devices and other equipment, one person asked, "Should we go ahead and set up for EVP?" A couple of digital recorders were already in operation, and when they were played back, in response to the question, an unidentified voice, believed to be a spirit, asked, "What is EVP?" Throughout the investigation, unexplained noises were detected, and EMF detectors indicated several spikes, including at the time of that recording. Another time, a digital recorder set up in the house for a period of time captured a voice saying, "Haaaauuuunted!" There were no people in the house at the time. So the ghost, apparently male, has a sense of humor and *knows* what he is.

The ghosts seem to be a bit picky about who they reveal themselves to, though. Volunteers at the museum often do not experience them, though there are exceptions. Guests and visitors seem to receive a lot of attention. Perhaps Mr. Korner and Mr. Milch are trying to entertain their guests.

Many people experience the feeling of being watched. Michael, Katie, Amy and Deonna all got this sense during their time in the house that day. Contracted workers seem to be the target of harmless pranks at times. Once, an HVAC tech was working on the top floor when he felt three distinct taps on his hat. There was no one else around. He gathered his tools and left immediately.

Deonna told us that Haunted NC had its first visit to the Folly in March or April 2010. Jim Hall, one of the team's investigators, received three taps while on the stage upstairs. He recorded a ten-degree temperature difference from the rest of his body. He was unaware of the original incident with the HVAC tech at the time.

Something unusual also happened in the grand reception room. The Haunted NC investigators did an experiment where they used an EMF meter. They would ask for the ghost to make the EMF meter spike to a number requested, and the meter would immediately indicate that number.

Many interesting things have been reported over the years. Footsteps were heard on the stairs. A woman was seen looking out a window when the house was empty. One woman who was inside saw a child in Victorian clothing on the front porch through the doors. A girlish giggle has been heard in the theater area.

The Folly wasn't always a private home. It served briefly as a funeral parlor and was even an antique store for a while. During this period, furniture would be rearranged when no one had been around. An interesting note here is that Korner was also a furniture maker, and he was known to be very particular about everything, including how furniture and other items were placed. Incidentally, 80 percent of the furniture in the Folly is the original furniture.

The Kernersville Little Theater has often used the Korner's Folly theater for productions. Many times, theater workers would turn off all the lights and leave only to notice one back on when they got outside. They would go back in and turn it off again. They also reported the smell of cigar smoke in areas of the house other than the smoking room set aside by Korner for that purpose. Investigators also noticed the smell in rooms far removed from the designated room. They discovered that Polly Alice had been a closet smoker. She probably sneaked a puff sometimes when Jule wasn't nearby.

Five to six different teams have done investigations in the Folly. Though there has been reported activity in most rooms and the cottage, a lot of it occurs in the front areas. Jule Korner Sr. died in the main bedroom, on the street level at the front of the house on Thanksgiving 1924. He, the houseguest Milch, Polly Alice, Aunt Dealy and several unknown children appear to be the main candidates for the ghosts. Interestingly enough, Michael asked Deonna how many actual spirits were supposed to be present. She, Michael and Katie all perked up immediately—there had been an actual aural response! Neither Michael nor Katie were certain

The main reception room. *Photo by Amy Spease.*

what was said. Deonna thought it was "five," but it was definitely a voice. Amy and a volunteer were the only others in the house at the time, and both of them were all the way upstairs at the time. Michael looked around, but the voice seemed to have come from thin air.

Michael felt the warmth and the welcoming feeling the others noted. Katie was amazed by the house. She noticed many antique items while she was walking around, including a couple of items similar to pieces she owns. She enjoyed her visit to the Folly very much. Amy said it was the most unique and wonderful place she has been to yet. She said the feelings of love and happiness present were almost like a welcoming embrace.

The spirits of Korner's Folly are not haunting it. They dwell there, happy in the place and in memories of times long past. They have a great sense of peace and remain because they love the old home, and each other, quite a lot.

Korner's Folly is open year round. Guided tours are scheduled by appointment seven days a week. Minimum group of ten and two weeks' notice are required for guided tours. Walk-in visitors are welcomed Thursday through Saturday, 10:00 a.m. to 4:00 p.m., and Sunday, 1:00 p.m. to 4:00 p.m. The foundation asks that visitors arrive an hour before closing. Admission is charged for adults and for children ages six to eighteen. Children under six are admitted for free. Please contact Korner's Folly for further details.

Korner's Folly
413 South Main Street; Kernersville, NC 27284
336-996-7922; www.KornersFolly.org
Executive Director: Mr. Bruce Frankel

The Legend of Aycock Auditorium

The old woman stood there, looking around the attic. A lifetime of memories and forgotten things were strewn about. As she gazed back through the mists of time to her long-ago youth, she reached up and pulled her long, gray hair down from the tight bun she usually wore these days. Absently, she stroked it, remembering how he had so loved her beautiful long hair and wanted her always to wear it down.

And his eyes! A melancholy smile crossed her lips as she thought of his clear blue eyes. Oh, how her heart had fluttered the first time he had turned those eyes upon her!

She remembered the hours they had spent together, falling in love. How proud she was of him in that new, crisp gray uniform! And she recalled the tears she'd cried the day he marched off with his regiment to the lilting tune of "Dixie."

As the days and then the months passed, she pined for her soldier and was thrilled by each letter she received. He described the conditions of the camps, fierce fighting that took her breath away and how he loved her so. She anxiously awaited the post every day but dreaded it almost as much. What if…

Then the awful day came. A letter said he was dead, killed bravely in battle defending the South. She refused to accept it. God would not allow her beloved to be taken from her. Her chest heaved as the tears of a lifetime ago flowed again. It had been over thirty-five years. She had never married—waiting and hoping…

UNCG's Aycock Auditorium. *Photo by Kristen Crutchfield Brown.*

But she could wait no longer. He wasn't coming back. She kicked the chair away and fell. The rope tied around her neck and the beam above caught her a foot from the floor, and she swung wildly to and fro. My God, how it hurt! She had not expected it to hurt so much. Her feeble hands clutched at the noose as her feet began to kick wildly. *NO!* Not like this! She'd find another way to go to him. Where was that chair?

Oh no! She saw it as she spun around. It was several feet away, lying on its side. The only hope was to get the rope from around her throat. Desperately, her fingers grasped at the ever-tightening rope. Her eyes bulged, and her lips worked as she gasped and struggled for air. As she spun, she saw her reflection in a dusty old floor-length mirror against the wall. Her face was turning purple.

Slowly, her kicking diminished and her fingers began to lose feeling. Finally, her hands fell limply to her sides and the kicking stopped. As she spun in a circle, a hand or foot would twitch now and then. She caught one final glimpse of herself in the mirror as everything began to fade to white.

No one knows for certain how long the poor old spinster dangled there, in the attic of her home on the corner of Spring Garden and Tate Streets. But everyone who knew her knew why she had done it. She had finally given up and gone to be with her lost Confederate soldier.

For a few years, people tried to live in the grand old Victorian home—first her relatives and then others. But no one stayed very long. For, you see, though they had cut her body down and buried her in the family plot, the poor woman's spirit remained in the house. At first they simply noticed things being moved around to places where the spinster had kept them. Then they began to smell a wafting perfume. This was easy enough to ignore. Scents linger for years, after all. But then the noises started. People in the house would hear footsteps on the stairs to the attic, though no one was visible on the steps. They retraced the poor woman's last climb to the attic. They would hear a woman crying, and an old rocking chair would move all by itself, back and forth.

Finally, her sad apparition appeared. She would look out a window or peer at them from a mirror. They even glimpsed her on the stairs now and then. This was too much. The house stood empty for a couple of decades, slowly deteriorating from neglect—empty, that is, but for the sad, lonely ghost of a little old lady.

The property was eventually sold to the North Carolina College for Women, now the coed University of North Carolina at Greensboro. The beautiful but dilapidated house was torn down to make way for a new campus theater. The theater was named Aycock Auditorium in honor of a governor of North Carolina. It opened in 1926.

It did not take long for rumors of a ghost to begin to spread. Yes, the spinster had moved into the new building. Students made up a name for her, according to Mr. Trojanowski, who teaches on the subject of campus ghosts at the university today. The students called her Jane and said she was the daughter of Governor Aycock. Thus the legend of Jane Aycock was born. To this day, the ghost is referred to as Jane.

The little old lady, however, was *not* Governor Aycock's daughter. Though he did have children, not one was named Jane. The students simply made up this backstory to give their resident spook a name. The name of the poor old spinster seems to have been lost to the ages. The ghost, however, doesn't seem to mind being called Jane. Whatever her name is, she remains active to this day. Her misty form has been seen many times across the decades, but she is more often heard or sensed than seen.

Faculty and students have experienced her activities many times over the many decades during which the theater has been open. Oftentimes, someone has lost or misplaced something only to have it reappear right where they'd left it. This seems to be one of the ghost's favorite tricks. She will also play the piano. Doors will be found open and unlocked when no one was there to do so, when people clearly remembered closing and locking them. Mostly, though, "Jane" loves to play with the lights. She'll turn them on and off.

Many a student and teacher have been suddenly plunged into total darkness by the spirit's antics, or someone might find himself or herself suddenly blinded by bright lights in their face.

The staff and students love their ghost and have given her a sign of respect for what she does. On the lighting control board, there is a switch labeled as "Jane's Dimmer." And despite the fact that they have her name wrong, the ghost loves to use "her" switch, for there is something particular about these controls. The lighting booth is located high up in the theater, in the precise location of the attic of the old house where the lonely spinster took her own life more than a century ago.

GREENSBORO COLLEGE GHOSTS

Greensboro College opened its doors as Greensboro Female College in April 1846. The school was renamed Greensboro College for Women in 1912 and, finally, simply Greensboro College in 1920. Men were first admitted as day students in 1954 and as residential students in 1956.

The beautiful, quaint campus sits in the heart of downtown Greensboro, just a block from the University of North Carolina–Greensboro. One might not suspect from the first look that the peaceful grounds harbor spirits of a haunted past. But at night, when shadows fall and the buildings grow quiet, something (or perhaps several somethings) roams the darkened halls.

The school's Main Building has suffered three major fires, in 1863, 1904 and 1941. Two of the fires have documented fatalities associated with them. The first death came in 1873, as reconstruction was nearing completion from the 1863 fire. A worker named William Barringer fell to his death from scaffolding. The second death occurred in the fall of 1941.

On September 9, 1941, in the midst of a severe storm, lightning struck the rotunda of Main Building. Mr. Henry McEntire, the school's treasurer, rushed to try to save college files and records from the spreading fire. As he desperately worked to get the records out, the roof collapsed around 1:20 a.m. The poor man was killed instantly.

There have been other deaths on campus as well. During the War for Southern Independence, a Confederate soldier passed away. The circumstances of his death are unclear. Some stories say he drowned in

Main Building, Greensboro College. *Photo by Michael Renegar.*

a pond that used to be on campus. Another story says he was crushed to death in a train accident on the railroad line near the library, and a third, most unlikely story, has him being killed while defending materials stored for reconstruction of the Main Building from Yankee invaders. The drowning story seems to be the most likely scenario. Whatever the circumstances of his death, the restless spirit of this "Johnny Reb" is said to linger, mostly around and inside the library. His singular form has been seen outside and near the old tracks, as well as in the stacks within the building.

In 1894, Dr. Dred Peacock became the college's seventh president. Sometime in the next few years, President Peacock's young daughter, Ethel, passed away in Main Building. This is perhaps one of the school's saddest tales. We do not know if Ethel died due to illness or accident, but her little apparition has been seen often, and she has also been heard and sensed in a third-floor hallway for many years.

There is an interesting anecdote concerning Ethel. After one of the fires, a portrait of Miss Ethel, among other important pieces of art and books, was sent to Greensboro College's sister school, Trinity College (later to become Duke University), for display and storage. Ethel's portrait and many other pieces were never returned. To this day, Greensboro College periodically requests return of the lost pieces, only to be told they cannot be found. According to legend, Miss Ethel Peacock's ghost is forever trapped in Main Building—at least until her portrait is returned to its rightful place.

In 1902, Mrs. Lucy H. Robinson succeeded Dr. Peacock as president of Greensboro College. She was the first woman to serve as the president of a college in the Southeast and, to date, is the only woman to hold the post at Greensboro College. She was president until 1913 but continued to be a presence on campus and a tireless supporter of the school. She died on campus, possibly in Main Building, on May 28, 1930. Her ghost is supposed to roam the halls of her beloved school, and today, she is most often noticed as an apparition seen out of the corners of the eyes or disappearing around corners in the hallways.

Some of the school's darkest hours fell upon the campus in 1918. That year, an influenza epidemic swept across the world, killing millions. Greensboro College was hit hard by the disease. The third floor of Main Building was quarantined as an infirmary for stricken students and faculty. We do not know how many of the ill succumbed to the flu; the records were destroyed in the 1941 fire. But their sad spirits are believed to linger up there as well.

The Parlor Theater opened in Main in 1986. The dark theater is said to be haunted by the ghost of one Mary Jane Swain Porter, who graduated from Greensboro College in 1850. She is better known as the mother of poet and writer Sydney Porter, also known as O. Henry. According to legend, if you begin talking about O. Henry in the theater, his mother will become active. She walks around, plays with the lights, makes noises and may even touch you. Workers in the building are told not to mention or discuss O. Henry in the theater, and many will not even go in the room alone.

Kristen Crutchfield Brown is a member of our ghost-hunting group, Camel City Spirit Seekers. She is also employed by Greensboro College and has an office in Main Building. She is an alumnus of the school, and she is the one who talked to the campus security chief, Chief Gilmore, and arranged for CCSS to do a paranormal investigation at the school.

Because the building is so big, we called upon our friend Bo Blackburn to bring some of his group as well. On May 1, 2010, we went to the campus.

In our group were Kristen, her mom, Ann, Amy and Michael. For Mystery Inc., those present were Bo, Jay, Ray, Tiffany and Angela.

While Amy, Kristen and Ann headed up to the third floor, the rest of us headed into the darkened theater. Ray and Tiffany went into the back rooms, and Bo walked around the theater while everyone else sat down. As Bo made EMF and temperature readings, Michael began an EVP session. Michael began asking a series of questions, addressing them to Mrs. Porter or any spirit present. It is always important to pause between each question to allow the spirit time to answer. The recommended time is five to fifteen seconds.

As time passed, Michael began talking about O. Henry and asking questions. As he read a couple of the man's poems, the air seemed to change somewhat around him. It felt thicker and cooler, and a charge seemed to be building the more he discussed O. Henry. At one point, he felt what seemed to be a pat on his shoulder, but there was no one near him. Temp readings taken just after he indicated the pat showed a five- to fifteen-degree difference in the air around his shoulder from other parts of the room.

Though he did feel the touch on his shoulder, the recordings later yielded no disembodied voices, and photos revealed nothing at the time. Bo later did catch what appears to be a seated figure when he was in there by himself. The photo is still under analysis.

Upstairs, however, the trio of women was having better results. Amy, Ann and Kristen sat down on the third-floor hallway allegedly haunted by Ethel Peacock. They began talking to the little girl, trying to coax her out. Amy began to see what appeared to be the little girl peering around a corner at them. After a while, the form slowly made its way up the hall toward them. Suddenly, Kristen said, "Something just sat down in my lap!"

Amy agreed. She could see a shimmering energy form, roughly the size of a child. It did indeed seem to be sitting in Kristen's lap. All three women said they saw Kristen visibly sink into the seat a little as if a child had climbed onto her lap. At this point, many people would probably have had enough and left. Not these three! They continued to try to engage Ethel, talking to her and inviting her to play. After several minutes, the spirit seemed to get up and move back down the hall.

Meanwhile, in another hallway, Ray, Angela and Michael, using magnetic devices brought by Bo, seemed to track a moving presence working its way down the main hallway. Tiffany joined them with a digital voice recorder. Efforts at aural communication came to naught, however, and the moving energy field eventually dissipated. They went back downstairs.

On the other hallway, the three women were preparing to leave. It was time to move over to the library. As Kristen was bidding the spirit goodbye, her digital voice recorder captured the best evidence of the night—a Class A EVP! Kristen was telling Ethel they were leaving and going to the library. As she said, "It is closer to West Market Street," a very clear childlike voice whispered, "Oh NO!"

We were all stunned and quite gratified to find this EVP later. It is clearly not one of the three women, and there was no one else up there with them at the time—no one living, anyway. They did capture another, fainter response earlier, but this was the "money shot."

The entire group then proceeded to the library. Amy took a smoke break, and Michael joined her at the "smoke bench" so she wouldn't be out there all by herself. The others had gone inside. As they sat there, both saw a shadow figure suddenly appear on the library wall. It lingered for a second and then vanished! It didn't move off like a person would have; it was just suddenly gone.

Inside, the group split up again, trying to roust the lonely Confederate soldier. At one point, Kristen saw a figure between her, Bo and Jay. Bo felt himself get knocked aside by an unseen force as Kristen snapped pictures. Though you can see Bo forcibly knocked against the wall in these photos, the soldier did not appear in the images. Try as we might, the Rebel never made himself known beyond this.

After this, we began to wind it down. Back in Main Building, Tiffany and Michael went to one of the back rooms of the theater she had investigated earlier. As Tiffany tried to contact a spirit, Michael took several photos. Some of these showed only blackness, despite his use of flash. Finally, Michael mentioned this, and Tiffany said, "I think she is doing that." After this, the photos showed the room as it should have with the flash.

We discussed the investigation later, and Amy said she saw at least five, possibly six, different spirits at varying times and places. Michael, of course, had the touch on his shoulder, as well as the incident with his camera. We decided the place was ripe for further investigation.

On December 14, 2010, Michael, Ann and Kristen returned to Greensboro College, along with Michael's mom, Katie, and a good friend, Jamie Dietz. Amy was unable to attend, and Bo's group was not there

Do spirits from the past linger in these halls? *Photo by Michael Renegar.*

either. This time, we concentrated our efforts on Ethel, the spirit who seemed to respond to us the most last time.

There were no chairs this time but two benches instead. Katie and Kristen sat down on one, and Michael and Jamie sat down on the one opposite them. Ann decided to sit on the floor. We began taking photos and trying to talk to Ethel. Try as we might, she would not make a visible appearance this time. However, she did make noises at the end of the hall, making it sound as if the door to the fire escape were opening and closing. All of us went down there at different times and heard the noises, but no one was at the door. At one point, we heard the sound of children running on the floor above. Kristen verified that this was impossible; that area of the attic was chock full of stored items. No one could have been walking up there, let alone running at full speed.

Ethel did seem to come out though. At one point, the belt on Katie's jacket came undone right in front of all of us. She didn't do it, and neither did any of the others. Other than that, though, not much happened on this visit. We believe Greensboro College is indeed haunted and warrants further study. If the administration and security are open to it, we wish to go back and continue our investigations at some point.

Ethel Peacock seems to be quite active at times, and President Robinson continues to be seen. Amy and Tiffany sensed at least one male spirit, too, besides the soldier in the library. Was this Mr. Barringer, Mr. McEntire or both? And what about those poor victims of the 1918 flu? We want to learn as much as we can and try to help them. If you go to Greensboro College, whether as a student, staff or visitor, keep an eye out. Not everyone you see may be a living, breathing person.

The Americans Fought Like Demons

Today, the United States of America and Great Britain are such fast friends that it is hard to imagine they were ever anything different. However, just 230 years ago at this writing, the two were locked in a struggle that would decide the very survival of the American state. For the thirteen colonies that formed the original United States were once a subject part of the British Empire, ruled from London by the monarch and Parliament.

Differences with the Crown government had been growing for years, but the colonials tried to maintain their relationship with the mother country. However, a series of chafing laws and taxation without representation in Parliament drove the colonies into open rebellion. By 1775, armed confrontation had taken place at Lexington and Concord, Massachusetts, setting in motion the American Revolution. The following July 4, 1776, the colonies formally renounced the Crown and declared their independence.

Declaring it and actually *winning* independence, however, would be two totally different things. The American Revolution was not, in its purest sense, a true revolution. When all was said and done, King George III still sat on the throne of Great Britain and Parliament was not toppled from power. America would be free and independent, so technically, it was a civil war. However, the new government formed by the American colonies *was* revolutionary. There would be no king or emperor and no royal family. The head of state would be an elected president. And the parliament, to be called Congress, would also be an assembly completely elected from the people,

Volunteers manned the first line of defense. *Photo by Michael Renegar.*

with no House of Lords whose membership in London was determined by dynastic traditions.

But first, there would have to be blood, and blood there was. The fledgling Continental army fought gallantly against the famed British redcoats (so named for their crimson uniforms) and their Hessian mercenary troops. But the Americans were ill equipped and lacked training, and the British and their hired German soldiers were among the best-trained armies in the world. Few in the capitals of Europe thought the Americans stood much of a chance.

There was a series of battles, some victories for the Americans and some stunning defeats. Lexington, Concord, Fort Washington and Fort Lee. Then, a breathtaking victory at Trenton, the day after Christmas 1776, followed by the heartbreaking defeat at Brandywine in September 1777.

In the northern colonies, the Americans had managed to fight the British to a draw, with neither army able to gain the upper hand. Then came the brutal winter of 1777–78, which nearly did what the British could not—

destroy the American army. Conditions were grave, and the military officers were continually frustrated by the Continental Congress's reluctance to send supplies. General George Washington, the supreme commander of the Continental army, was deeply concerned for the state of his army and whether it would be in any shape to resume hostilities. His quartermaster general, Nathanael Greene, worked the Congress and roundly cursed the Congress and managed, somehow, to keep the army from starving at the winter quarters at Valley Forge.

Major General Nathanael Greene was a native of Rhode Island and had served Washington faithfully since the beginning of the war. He had mistakenly pushed Washington to try to hold Forts Washington and Lee and was blamed for their loss. However, Washington kept faith with Greene. He was in command of one division of the Continental army in the Battle of Monmouth, New Jersey, as the army departed winter quarters.

In August, Greene was sent to Rhode Island with French nobleman the Marquis de Lafayette. There, they were to coordinate an assault with French admiral Comte d'Estaing. The French, ever England's enemy, had seen an opportunity in the conflict and allied themselves with the American colonies. This campaign, however, ended in defeat for the Allies, and Greene returned to Washington and the main army.

In June 1780, Washington placed Greene in charge of the army that defeated the British at the Battle of Springfield. That August, General Greene resigned as quartermaster general. He cited the continuing interference with military affairs by the Continental Congress. Washington assigned him to duty at West Point, New York, home of the U.S. Military Academy. In September, he was the presiding judge at the court-martial that sent British spy Major John Andre—who was said to have conspired with American traitor General Benedict Arnold—to the gallows.

On August 16, 1780, British forces under General Charles, Earl Cornwallis attacked the American southern army, under General Horatio Gates, near Camden, South Carolina. The Americans were routed, with the army breaking apart and running in total confusion. The southern army was effectively destroyed, and the way was clear for General Lord Cornwallis to rally his forces, join with Loyalists (known as Tories) in the Carolinas and invade Virginia. He planned to secure the ports on the coast and then bring in more troops to secure the South.

Congress had finally seen the error of its ways in trying to run the military. A succession of generals it had handpicked had lost Savannah, Georgia, and Charleston, South Carolina, and then suffered the fiasco at Camden. The Congress decided to place the military decisions in Washington's hands, rubber stamping whatever he decided to do. The general immediately chose General Greene to take full command of the Southern Department. He would have extraordinary full powers, subject only to Washington himself. The general departed West Point to take charge of his command.

General Greene arrived in Charlotte on December 2, 1780, and took survey of his army. The southern army was in pitiful shape. The British had whipped them badly at Camden, morale was low and supplies were short. And marching toward them was a vastly superior force under Cornwallis.

Despite this, Greene decided, incredibly, to divide his army, thus forcing the British general to divide his forces as well. The strategy worked. Even as Cornwallis took Charlotte, the tide was about to turn. A force of Loyalists was defeated by a force made up largely of colonial militia at Kings Mountain, North Carolina. Shortly thereafter, on January 17, 1781, one of Greene's columns, under Brigadier General Daniel Morgan, scored a resounding victory at Cowpens, South Carolina, killing or capturing nine out of ten of the British troops sent against him.

Greene had sent half his force northward under his second in command, Brigadier General Isaac Huger. Greene himself united with Morgan's division north of Charlotte. He decided to retreat and gather more forces before engaging the British head-on. He wrote to Huger to join him at Guilford Courthouse, from which they would continue the strategic retreat until they were strong enough to face Cornwallis. Thus began the famous "Race to the Dan River."

Major General Lord Cornwallis was frustrated. He had been raised on the battlefields of Europe, where lines of men marched onto the field and blasted at one another from perfectly organized battle lines. He did not like the way things transpired here. But as the southern army, his direct opponent, was moving northeast, he had little choice but to follow. His army was beset by troubles. When they crossed the Yadkin River at Shallow Ford, the river was swollen from rains and delayed Cornwallis severely. In modern-day Davidson County, he was again delayed and, to add insult to injury, was forced to leave much of the spoils he had taken behind, sinking the treasure in Abbots Creek.

According to legend, a soldier was killed as they unloaded the barrels of loot, crushed by one of them. His ghost is said to linger at the spot on Abbots Creek and watch over Cornwallis's treasure. (It seems clear that any treasure was either retrieved or reclaimed long ago.)

In the meantime, Greene had arrived at Guilford on February 9 and called for his officers. He asked if they should stand and fight. After a discussion and vote, it was decided to continue to retreat and gather strength. Greene created a special light corps under Colonel Otho Williams to cover the retreat and moved north again. His army numbered just over 2,000 men, about 1,400 of them Continental regulars and the rest Carolina militia.

By February 10, Cornwallis and his army had reached the Moravian settlement of Salem, about twenty-five miles from Guilford Courthouse. The Americans moved again, and by the fourteenth, they had crossed the Dan River at Irvine's Ferry in Halifax County, Virginia. They had outrun the British and now began to make ready for battle.

More militia forces joined the colonials, and they remained on the north side of the Dan for only a week. General Greene was ready to take on Lord Cornwallis. His army crossed the Dan again on February 22, 1781, and returned to North Carolina. The British had lingered at Salem, but Cornwallis and his forces were eager to confront the enemy. When he learned Greene was on the move, General Lord Cornwallis set his army to preparing for the battle he knew would come. When he heard that the southern army was setting up at Guilford Courthouse, he began to march.

The sun rose on a bright and clear day on March 15, 1781. It was rather cool still, though. The British were resplendent in their crimson redcoat uniforms and white pants. The mercenary regiment, hired from a Hessian prince in Germany, wore the Prussian blue uniform coats preferred by several of the northern German armies. The Continental forces wore blue for the regulars and pretty much anything they could lay hands on for the militia.

The British army, numbering 1,900 men, was moving up the Great Road (now called New Garden Road, after the Quaker community that was founded in the area). General Greene had set up his now much larger force of 4,400 men in three lines across the Great Road. The first, southernmost line was made up mostly of the Carolina and Virginia militia and had a pair of cannon set up right in the road. A few regulars and state troops were placed with them. The militia men were notoriously skittish and known for running. Based on past experience, Greene told the militia troops that they were required to fire only two volleys before breaking ranks. He then turned to the regulars assigned to be with the militia and told them in front of the volunteers to shoot anyone who broke ranks before firing *both* volleys required of them.

The first line of defense stood ready at the northern end of a clearing about half a mile from the courthouse and Greene's last line. The steady beat of the drums announced the approach of Cornwallis's forces. Soon, the perfectly dressed lines of British and Hessian infantry came into view, along with a force of mounted dragoons. Flags fluttered in the breeze, and the thump of the drums and marching feet sent a vibration through the militiamen. They grew nervous but held their ground. It was an impressive sight to see the redcoats marching steadily forward. The British halted and fired their first volley at about 12:30 p.m. The militiamen responded, and the battle was on.

The militia forces proved up to the task assigned and actually held for forty-five minutes, firing far more than the two volleys required of them. But the better-trained European troops were just too much and broke through the line's center and advanced. While the militia melted away from the center, forces in the woods on each side of the road continued to keep the redcoats under heavy fire for some time.

The second line of Colonial forces waited 350 yards farther north in thick underbrush and heavy woods. The British reached this line of soldiers around 1:15 p.m. On this line, the fighting was close and fierce, some even hand to hand. The mounted troops of Cornwallis's army were basically useless here. After about an hour's bloodbath, the royal army finally broke through and came into a third clearing.

At the northern edge of this clearing stood Greene's main force of regulars. They were well rested and chafing for a fight. The British were tired and bloodied, and even the common soldiers on the field had noticed their numbers were dwindling. As the British moved to engage the third line, the colonials charged and forced them back.

But this was the best-trained army in the world that the colonials were facing. The British pushed forward, and the colonials gave ground. The British captured Greene's field artillery and turned it on them. At this point, Washington's legion charged the British infantry, and the battle descended into a chaotic melee. The fighting was ferocious and was close quarters, with the British and colonials mixing together in a heaving mass of men.

Taking one look at this bloody scene, General Lord Cornwallis ordered the artillery to load grapeshot and fire it directly into the roiling mass of humanity. He knew full well his own soldiers would be hit as well, but thought it better to break this up as quickly as possible. Volley after volley of the scrap metal called grapeshot blasted into the massed fighting men. Englishmen fell beside Americans. Finally, the forces separated, leaving a moaning, bloody pile of dying men and body parts.

General Greene chose to withdraw at this point, leaving the field to Cornwallis. The colonials marched about fifteen miles away and halted to regroup. Cornwallis declined to pursue, as his army was decimated. Greene didn't like leaving the British with yet another victory but was pleased with how his soldiers had acquitted themselves. He was particularly proud of the militia, which had held far longer than he'd thought it would.

Cornwallis, however, was not pleased at all with the outcome. Yes, he held the field, but it was a pyrrhic victory. Of his force of 1,900 who started the battle, 532 were now dead—over one-fourth of his whole army, with hundreds more wounded. These men were irreplaceable, as was much of the equipment lost. Greene lost only 268 of his men. The losses to the British were so drastic that a British official was said later to have quipped, "Any more such victories shall ruin the British Empire!"

Since they held the field of battle, the British also were left to deal with the aftermath of the carnage. They would have to collect and see to the injured, as well as bury the dead. The cries of the wounded rang throughout the night, keeping the already beleaguered British and Hessians from desperately needed sleep.

The next morning, after breakfast, the redcoats set about the grim task of burying the dead. Corpses lay everywhere. Some were buried where they lay, but most were heaped together in massive graves and buried with no markers. This task completed, General Lord Cornwallis decided to march to Wilmington, North Carolina, to resupply his battered army.

Greene watched and waited. When it became clear where Cornwallis was headed, he relaxed somewhat and set about tending to his soldiers and resupplying them. After resupplying, the British marched to Virginia to begin what was supposed to be Cornwallis's push to secure the South. This was not to be, however. As soon as the British were firmly in Virginia, Greene moved south, steadily retaking areas Cornwallis had captured and placed under the British flag. The Americans would secure the South instead of the British, and Cornwallis's army would end up surrounded at Yorktown, Virginia, in September 1781. General Washington himself soon arrived, and more than twenty thousand American troops, bolstered by their French allies, were arrayed against the British. The hammer fell when a fleet of French warships and troopships arrived off the coast by Yorktown. Cornwallis's troops made a valiant effort to break out, but it was the endgame. In October, General Lord Cornwallis surrendered his command to General Washington. For all intents and purposes, the war was over.

The Battle of Guilford Courthouse was a turning point in the Revolution and was a truly bloody engagement. Asked about it later, retired General Charles, Earl Cornwallis replied without hesitation, "I have never seen such fighting since God made me. The Americans fought like demons!"

Today, houses, apartments and businesses occupy much of the land on which the battle was fought. These buildings stand on ground where many men fell and over several unmarked mass graves. It should come as no surprise, with the violence and large number of men killed, that there are many ghost stories about the battlefield and the surrounding area.

Guilford Courthouse National Military Park owns about one-fifth of the total battlefield area today. James and Jenny are a young couple Michael knows from a former job. They live in Greensboro now and often visit the park, as James is a history aficionado. One visit, however, was a little different. It was in February.

"We were sitting on a bench, talking and discussing Nathanael Greene and the battle," James told me. "And I had just told Jenny that Greene went south after the battle, and she was saying he'd moved off northward and joined Washington for the final victory at Yorktown."

"Here comes a reenactor, let's see if he can settle this," Jenny said.

James said he looked up and saw a man approaching in a red uniform. He thought it must be one of the hundreds of reenactors who come to the park every March to re-create the battle. "Man!" Jenny said as he drew closer. "Look at that uniform! He's got it pretty authentic!"

Indeed, James said, it did look authentic. The red uniform was dirty and tattered. There appeared to be a spot of blood over the right breast of the uniform. "Excuse me," Jenny said as he walked up to them, "could you settle something for us?"

The man did not stop and did not say a word. In fact, he kept on walking as if he hadn't heard a word. Jenny was incensed and jumped up, yelling, "Hey! That was rude, Man! I was talking to you!"

James said the man did turn around then, but they wished he hadn't, for his eyes were totally devoid of life or emotion. Jenny sat down, feeling suddenly ill, and James said that an unnatural chill fell over them. And there was a stench of gunpowder, blood and rot about them. James said Jenny's mouth was moving, trying to form words, but she was speechless with fear and had turned quite white. James said he then recognized the uniform as that of a soldier of the Seventy-first Highlanders. The Scotsman looked at them for a second and then, without making a sound, turned and walked a few steps before vanishing into thin air. The couple didn't return to the park for a few weeks and never did go back to that particular area.

Apparently, encounters of this type happen with some regularity, both with ghostly British soldiers and colonials. Park officials are often asked about reenactors roaming the park when, in fact, no reenactors have been present on those occasions. A couple of people have even reported lines of soldiers standing, dressing (evening out and straightening) their lines as if in preparation for acting out the battle. They were also told that no reenactors were present in the park.

Many years ago, there were also some strange reports from the neighboring apartments about the noise of horses in the park at night. However, horses have never been kept at the park, and no signs of such animals were found after these reports, which peaked and ended in the 1970s. No explanation was ever found for these nightly echoes of the past.

One of the most haunted areas of the park is where General Greene's third line stood near the courthouse itself. A statue of Nathanael Greene, atop his horse, sits in this area. The most intense fighting of the battle occurred in this area. It is where Cornwallis's artillery famously fired grapeshot into the hopelessly mixed colonists and royal soldiers. People—including Jenny—often report feeling suddenly very ill in this area of the park. They also report deep chills and intense feelings of fear and sorrow. A few have said they felt as if hundreds of unseen eyes were watching them. And the sound of bagpipes can often be heard floating across the clearings and through the trees, even when there are no bands present. We do know that at least one unit of Highlanders fought in the battle, soldiers of the Seventy-first Highlanders Regiment.

Rangers used to live in the park in a building called Quarters Two. Some reported being kept awake at night by strange voices, footsteps and other noises, yet when they investigated, the area was invariably quiet and empty but for them. These recurring noises were heard inside and outside the house.

The visitors' center and superintendent's house stand on New Garden Street, which was once the Great Road and was the main route taken by the marching British that March day in 1781. Objects such as tools were said to move of their own volition in the superintendent's house. It has been unoccupied as a residence for some time now. Incidents have also been reported in the visitors' center. A giant painting of General Greene resides there, close to the main desk. Some swear the painting is haunted and that it will watch you. Uneasy feelings are said to suddenly fall upon people who are alone near the painting. One employee said she felt as if someone were standing right beside her, watching her, as she worked alone one evening. She left rather quickly.

There is also allegedly a ghost of more recent vintage in the building. A longtime employee retired and passed away a short time later. He always wore his keys on a chain attached to his belt. He had a lot of keys, and they jingled rather loudly when he walked. Shortly after the man died, people who knew him began to hear the sound of his jingling keys. No one was really scared by this, however, as they had known the man and feel he is a friendly spirit.

One woman—we'll call her Sally, since she didn't want her name used—used to live in the Battle Forest Apartments. She discovered one night that she wasn't alone in her first-floor digs. "I had been having strange feelings of cold, even when I had the temperature set to eighty degrees," Sally told Michael, "and I would put my keys down on the table and walk away. Then when I would go to grab them, they would be gone. I would find them hanging on a hook I put up by the fridge every time."

Then one night, around 1:00 a.m., she was awakened by a loud noise. At first she thought there might be a prowler, but the apartment was completely silent. She listened intently for a moment, but nothing else happened. Deciding she'd just imagined the noise, Sally got up to go to the bathroom. Then, she decided she was thirsty. As she went to the kitchen, she began to get a sense that she wasn't alone. Before she could react, a man stood before her out of nowhere! She screamed, and the man reacted. He smiled sheepishly, tipped his three-cornered hat and then vanished before her eyes. The terrified woman ran for her bed and dove under the covers. As soon as she stopped shaking, she called 911 and reported a prowler. The police came but could find no sign of anyone who didn't belong, nor could they find any sign of forced entry. One of the officers told her that this happened sometimes in these apartments. When he asked her what the man was wearing, Sally told him a blue uniform top, white pants and a black hat. The officer then told her it was probably the ghost of one of the colonial soldiers killed in the Battle of Guilford Courthouse.

Sally did some research and found out that the apartments not only stood on part of the battlefield but that there was also likely one or more mass graves there. Her ghostly visitor never made another appearance—at least not to Sally. She found another apartment across town within weeks and moved, thus denying him the chance to show himself to her again.

And finally, we have reports from the 1800s of not one but *two* ghosts, the most clichéd type of all—headless horsemen. Two cavalry soldiers of

Continental army reenactors. *Photo by Michael Renegar.*

the Light Horse Guards were killed near a tree that had been uprooted. The hole left by the tree was just too tempting to pass up for the British soldiers on burial detail. They rolled the two lifeless corpses into the hole and buried the two men by cutting the tree and letting the stump and roots fall back. A road was built by the forgotten grave sometime later, and soon, stories began to make the rounds that the road was haunted. The two dead mounted soldiers were said to be seen riding down the road at night. They would come galloping at a breakneck pace, clearly recognizable in their crimson uniforms, not seeing where they were going, for they had no heads! For years, this road was not very busy at night at all.

The war ended, but animosity between the two countries did not immediately go away. In 1812, the two cousin nations fought another war, this time largely over British practices at sea. The British would manage to burn Washington, D.C., but lost this conflict as well. Had the English been able to devote their full attention to this war, the United States might not exist as such today. They were distracted, however, by a greater war closer to home. They were joining the Russian tsar and other European nations in what amounted to a world war against the French emperor and military genius Napoleon Bonaparte. Coincidentally, one of the British regiments engaged against the "Little Corporal" was the Thirty-third—Cornwallis's old regiment, soon to be dubbed Wellington's Regiment—which had fought at Guilford Courthouse.

Today, the differences of the past are long faded, and America and Britain stand firmly at each other's side, each ready to jump in front of the proverbial train for the other. Two world wars have sealed this bond forever. But echoes of that long-ago violent quarrel still linger at Guilford Courthouse National Military Park and its surrounding area. One might wonder how all those men who died would feel about the close relationship that their countries, once sworn blood enemies, now share.

Dana Auditorium

Dana Auditorium is a wonderful old theater on the campus of Guilford College. The school was founded in 1837 as the New Garden Boarding School by the Quaker settlers in their New Garden community. Later, in 1888, it was reestablished as Guilford College.

The city of Greensboro is home to a large Quaker community. New Garden, which had been settled before the American Revolution, was absorbed into the city when it became the county seat of Guilford County in 1808. When first established, the name was spelled "Greensborough" and was named for General Nathanael Greene, who led the colonial forces at the nearby Battle of Guilford Courthouse. According to tradition, Dana Auditorium is built on the site of a field hospital set up to receive the wounded and dying from that fight. A YMCA, built in 1891, occupied the site for many years.

Philanthropist Charles A. Dana made donations to Guilford College, and several new buildings were added to the campus in the early 1960s. One of these was Dana Auditorium, which was named for the donor. Dana has a long history of ghostly legends, almost from its opening day. Most of these stories involve a spectral soldier of Revolutionary vintage that staff and students call "Lucas." Since the majority of activity reported occurs in the wee hours of the morning, campus security officers are the usual subjects of Lucas's antics. The diligent ghost accompanies them on their rounds in the building and has been known to play tricks on them.

Often, the guards will notice lights burning when they know for certain that they had turned them off and that no one else was in the building. Sometimes, Lucas will make a game of this, keeping the guards occupied with the lights for several turns before letting them off the hook.

Lucas must have been a musician in his army life. One of his favorite tricks is to tickle the ivories in the choir room. When a guard comes to check and see who is playing the piano, the music stops as he opens the door. Often, the last note will still be sounding as the guard enters, though no one is there! Though he may play any of the several pianos present, Lucas's favorite instrument seems to be one particular piano that sits on a raised section of the floor.

Students and other staff are not immune to Lucas's activities. In 1991, Robert was a student at Guilford College, and he would often be in Dana Auditorium until very late at night. On one particular occasion, he was in the building alone. As he walked down a hallway, he clearly heard footsteps behind him. He turned, but no one was there. He continued to walk, and the footsteps behind him resumed. When he would stop, the other footfalls

Haunted theaters are a theme on Triad college campuses. *Photo by Michael Renegar.*

would stop, then start back when he did. Robert rounded a corner, stopped short and raced back around the corner, thinking he would catch someone playing a trick on him. No one was in the hall, but the sound of the footsteps continued, walking right at him! Robert left the building then, leaving his books where they were. He would hear the ghostly footsteps many more times during his stay at Guilford College.

While Lucas seems to be the most active spirit, others are said to haunt Dana Auditorium. Many people say that the spirit of a little girl also roams the building when things are quiet. Robert thinks he caught a glimpse of this elusive spirit one night in the auditorium itself. He saw a small figure out of the corner of his eye that he thought was a child. Wondering what a young girl was doing there, he turned to speak to her. But when he looked directly at the spot where he'd noticed the figure, there was no one there. Others have claimed to see this little girl's shade. Some say the vision is quite disturbing—for the child has no face. This spirit is said to be rather unpleasant, even mean. A feeling of cold and fear often accompanies an appearance by her.

One more serious incident is said to have occurred in the late 1970s, though we were unable to verify details. Two guards were working in the building. They had locked the doors, and no one else was around. As they walked in the auditorium, they heard a loud "swishing" sound. Both guards looked up instinctively and saw, to their complete amazement, one of the huge chandeliers, made of crystal, swinging back and forth. As the two men watched, the chandelier swung faster and faster. Suddenly, the chandelier snapped free from the ceiling and crashed to the seats below, shattering into a million pieces. This incident was blamed on Lucas by several people. However, others believe that the destruction of the chandelier was the work of the mysterious faceless girl. Indeed, it seems more in line with the character of the petulant little girl than the playful Lucas.

Another ghost seen in the auditorium may be someone else entirely, or it may be a visual manifestation of Lucas; we just aren't sure. One guard described an incident in which he confronted this ghost. As he was doing his rounds in Dana, he saw a man in a long overcoat standing in the hallway. The man was wearing a wide-brimmed, floppy hat down over his brow, obscuring his face. When the guard confronted the man, demanding to know who he was, the figure turned promptly and walked directly *through* the wall into a room called the Moon Room. The guard walked out of the building right away. Was this Lucas? Was it one of his compatriots from the battle? Or was it someone of a completely different origin? Only the ghosts know for sure, and they don't seem to be spilling their thoughts to anyone.

These are just some of Dana Auditorium's ghostly residents. With a building so old, built over historic ground, there is little wonder that ghostly goings-on are reported. If you happen to drop by Guilford College when you visit Greensboro and find yourself in Dana Auditorium, say "Hello!" to Lucas and his fellow spirits. Who knows? They may reply or play one of their famous tricks on you.

The Lonely Girl

April 2006

Amy was driving to pick up a photo disc from a shoot she'd done a few weeks earlier. She got off Interstate 40 and moved along down High Point Road. As she approached Jamestown, she began to have a funny feeling. Had she been here before?

Down the hill ahead, she saw a railroad underpass, and the feeling of familiarity grew stronger. Just before going under the bridge, she looked to her left and saw an older underpass covered in ivy and vines. Her heart skipped a beat as she realized where she was. This was Lydia's bridge!

Amy pulled over to the side of the road after clearing the underpass and sat thinking. How had she wound up here without realizing it? Her mind recalled all the old stories about the bridge and the lonely ghost said to linger there. She looked at the directions written down on a scrap of paper and realized that she had taken a wrong turn. She had been so sure this was the way she was supposed to go, but why? Had the poor girl from long ago somehow reached out to her sensitive mind and drawn her here? She shook her head, carefully got back on the road and headed back toward the interstate.

The original Jamestown underpass. *Photo by Michael Renegar.*

1923(?)

The lovely young woman smiled up at her dashing suitor, her long gown swishing as they danced to the band. She was so happy! He smiled back at her, and all the world seemed to exist in a distant realm. But it was getting late. "What time is it?" she asked.

The young man pulled out his pocket watch and looked. "Oh my," he replied. "It's about 11:30."

The young woman groaned. She was having such a good time! But she'd promised her mother she would be home before too late. "I'm having a lovely time," she told him, "but I promised Mother. We have to be going."

To his credit, the young man only allowed his smile to falter for a second. "All right, Dear," he said, "I'll go get our coats. Meet me by the door."

She waited by the door, looking through the windows. It had started to rain. Great! They'd have to drive slower than normal! Her date arrived, his coat already on, and helped her into hers. "It's pouring out there!" he observed, "but don't worry, Sweetheart, I'll get you home as quickly as I can."

The girl waited as he dashed out and pulled the car to the door. She covered her head with her scarf, took a deep breath and ran out, jumping into the passenger seat of the Ford. "I'm getting your seat all wet!" she gasped.

"It'll dry," he replied. "Not so sure about that dress, though."

The girl giggled as he pulled away. They were mostly quiet as they drove along, occasionally speaking about their plans for the future or what certain members of their families or friends might be doing. But they grew silent as the rain intensified and a thick fog began to roll in. He could barely see three feet in front of the car, but he was driving faster than he should be, not wanting to get her in trouble with her mother.

They never saw it coming as they approached the underpass on U.S. 29/70 near Jamestown. One instant they were a happy couple, on their way home from a dance. The next, there was a huge crash, and she was stumbling from the car and falling at the side of the road by the underpass. Through the driving rain, she looked back into the car. He was clearly dead, his blank eyes wide open, his head against the steering wheel. Tears streamed down her face, mixing with the cold rain.

She tried to take a step, but pain shot up her leg. She looked down. Blood was flowing from a terrible gash in her leg. Her dress was ripped, and blood also covered her abdomen. Suddenly, her head was throbbing. She touched her hand to her head and pulled it away to look. Her hand was covered in blood as well. Steam rose from the scene, and the world began to spin. As she fell, the young woman's last word was a mournful, "Mama!" The world faded to black.

1924

Rain was coming down steadily. "Burke Hardison" was driving home to High Point from Raleigh. It had been a long trip, and he was looking forward to getting home. He could just feel his bed beneath his tired back as he drove down U.S. 29/70 toward Jamestown. Suddenly, through the rain and fog, his headlights caught a bright vision. There was a young girl standing by the side of the road at the railroad underpass. She was wearing a long white formal gown. "What in the world?" he wondered as he slowed down and stopped beside her. He reached over and rolled the window down. "What are you doing out here, young lady?" he asked.

In a very soft voice, she replied, "I was at a dance, and we had an accident. Can you please take me home? I live in High Point."

"That's where I'm headed now," he answered, opening the door. "Jump in, and I'll take you home."

With a grateful nod, the young woman climbed into the vehicle beside him. He asked her name, and she told him in a soft, distant voice. She sounded hollow and miles away. Had she said Lydia was her name? He wasn't sure. She gave him her address, and he was somewhat aware of where it was. Slowly, he pulled back onto the road and headed toward High Point.

As they drove, Burke tried to engage the strange young woman in conversation, but she was reluctant to talk. Finally, she turned her head toward the window and said, "My mother will be worried. Why do you ask me all these questions? Please, just take me home."

The fellow gave up. She obviously didn't want to talk. They made the rest of the trip in silence. When they pulled up to the house she had directed him to, she paused, as if she were having trouble with the door. Burke gallantly jumped out of the vehicle and ran around the car, opening the passenger door. But to his amazement, all that he saw in the car was a puddle of water on the seat.

Hmmm, where did she go? He hadn't seen her get out. Scratching his head, he turned and walked up to the house. He decided he'd better see that she was all right. He stepped up on the porch and knocked on the door. Within seconds, the porch light came on, and an older lady answered the door. Burke did not notice the look of sad resolve on her face. "Hello, ma'am," he said. "I just brought a young lady here; she got gone before I could say anything. Just wanted to check and see that she made it inside all right."

Now he saw the sadness in her eyes, and he became quite confused at her tears. "Yes, yes, I know," she replied, in a voice filled with sorrow. "That was my daughter. She was killed in an accident out there at that underpass. You aren't the first one to try to bring her home to me. She just never seems to make it. But thank you for your trouble."

Burke was left standing there, gaping in disbelief as the old woman shut the door and turned out the light. After a few moments, he turned, descended the steps and went to his vehicle. He sat there in stunned silence for a few minutes more and then drove away. But he would never forget the night he took the lonely girl home. Years later, he recalled it as if it were yesterday when interviewed by Nancy Roberts for her first book on North Carolina ghost stories. He begged her not to use his real name because he didn't want the ridicule that he'd known when he first told the story. Thus she dubbed him with the pseudonym "Burke Hardison," which most writers since have written him as, never knowing it wasn't his true name. To this day, only Mrs. Roberts Brown, her husband Bruce and the man's descendants know who he really was.

THE PRESENT

Thus the legend of Lydia's Bridge was born. The story has been repeated and embellished over the years and is one of North Carolina's most well-known and beloved ghost stories. Others have claimed to have seen her or picked her up over the years. In the 1930s, the story inspired local teenagers to perpetrate a hoax at the underpass, dressing up one of them as a "ghost" in a long dress and scaring passersby by attempting to jump on the running boards of their cars or acting like they were reaching for their door handles.

Through the '50s and '60s, she was seen, with a few people claiming to have picked her up and attempted to take her home. Even when the road was re-routed and a new underpass was built, making the terrible curve less severe, the story persisted. The ghost, known as Lydia because of that first story, simply moved the few dozen yards to the new underpass when cars no longer passed the one where she is supposed to have died. Tom Beasely of High Point saw her there in the late '70s as he and a friend drove home late one night. They did not pick her up, though he told me later that if he had it to do over again, she would have gotten in and they would have seen if the girl they saw was a ghost or not.

Over the years, many people have tried to find out who this poor Lydia really was. Linda Headstrom at the High Point Library's North Carolina Room did a lot of research. She tracked down every single woman named Lydia who died in Guilford County in 1923. Unfortunately, she discovered that not a single one of them fit the legend. One of the Lydias they found was an infant, and all the others died of illnesses ranging from meningitis to tuberculosis and heart disease. One death record was missing—one Lyddie M. Underweood. Later, a fellow researcher, and then Michael on his own, located this death certificate as well. Miss Underwood was also an infant when she died, so she couldn't possibly be the girl of legend either.

Though this appeared to be the end of the story, other researchers contended that maybe Lydia had died earlier or later than 1923. So the search was on! Becky Allison, who was a member of our group before moving on to start her own, spent hours relentlessly searching for Lydia. She checked everywhere. However, between 2007 and 2011, every single woman named Lydia who died in Guilford County between 1900 and 1940 was accounted for. None of them fit the story, and none of them died at that underpass. Becky finally gave up after searching page after page of death records.

Some controversy continues concerning one Lydia Jane M______, who one man claims was born in 1904 and died December 31, 1923. He says she was nineteen and was killed in a car wreck. Unfortunately, this isn't true. The only Lydia who died on that date was Lydia Jane McCarthy. She was one of the women located by the High Point Library, and her actual death certificate shows that she was born in 1847 and was seventy-six when she died. The cause of death was clearly recorded: heart disease.

With this proven false, others insisted her name was Lydia Jane *Something*. Several independent researchers separately *did* find a Lydia Jane who died in a car accident, but it happened in January 1921 in the Proximity community of Greensboro, miles from the underpass. This was Lydia Jane Fields, a sixty-year-old widow who was struck by a car as she walked in the city. Again, not our young debutante at Jamestown. She was the only Lydia Michael found who died in any form of car accident in that forty-year time period.

Michael began collecting ghost stories in the late 1980s and began planning a book in 1995. He talked to several elderly people who had lived in and around High Point and Greensboro in 1923. A few actually remembered several accidents at the underpass, some of which were fatal. A few also remembered an accident that took the life of a young woman at the underpass. Two thought this occurred in 1923, and one thought it was earlier, maybe as early as 1911. However, all agreed that the name of the girl killed was definitely *not* Lydia. They could not recall the exact name, but Michael was told it was Mary, Marion, Mary Anne or something of that nature.

This opens up a whole new can of worms. There were a whole lot more women named Mary who died in Guilford County in the time period than there were Lydias. Looking through all those is a monumental task that could take years. Anyone who wants to tackle the task, have at it!

The name Mary does have some evidential support. The late Frances Casstevens says this story is the basis for the bluegrass song "Bringing Mary Home" by the Country Gentlemen and its sequel, "I've Come to Take You Home." Also, an EVP recorded at the underpass a couple of years ago caught a woman's voice saying what sounds like Mary in response to a question about a name. Several male voices are also heard, however.

One anecdote Michael received also could support the name Mary as that of the ghost, if it is true. A woman who used to live in High Point claimed she lived in a house on Johnson Street. She reported seeing the ghost of an elderly lady on a few occasions in the house. In the first incident, she arrived home late one night, and as her ride's headlights crossed the front of her house, she saw a woman pull aside the curtains and look out. She assumed it was her mom until she got inside and found everyone fast asleep. She saw the woman again in the living room, where the spirit said, "You look like my Mary," and then vanished. She also saw the ghost in her room late one night as she lay in bed. The ghost demanded, "What are you doing in my Mary's bed?" The woman then began asking the neighbors, who told her that an elderly widow did live in the house at one time—and that her daughter had died in a car wreck many years before. Eureka, right?

Not exactly. While it does fit our legend quite well, we could not find the particular address on Johnson Street that the woman gave Michael. There wasn't a number even close. Perhaps the street numbers have been redone; we just don't know. And the woman has dropped out of contact with us, leaving some doubt in our minds. The only reason we include her anecdote is because Johnson Street is actually one of the many streets associated with the Lydia legend over the years. We have heard it before, as well as Forest, Walnut, Woodleaf, Maple and even Centennial Street. Research shows that Lydia Fields lived on Maple Street.

This leaves an interesting question. Upon looking back, we found some very early reports about the story. In these early accounts, either the girl is not named or the name Mary is given. Did Lydia Fields's name somehow get mixed up in the story?

We think it is possible, since one account says the ghost lived on Maple Street. We know Ms. Fields did live on Maple Street in Gilmer Township. It is entirely plausible that someone remembered this unfortunate woman's name and that she died in a car crash. For some reason, by accident or design, they associated the underpass story with her, and BOOM! The legend of Lydia grew.

We are *not* stating that this is a fact, but it is as plausible a possibility as anything we have heard. But one thing we can say with the support of historical records. *No one, absolutely no one, named Lydia ever died out at the Jamestown Underpass.* Research has proven this to be irrefutable fact, unless someone can produce an as-yet-undiscovered death certificate. Perhaps the girl's name was Mary. Probably, even. Perhaps it was something entirely different. We will likely never know.

Another possibility is that all the attention to the area over the years has attracted a spirit or spirits from sites close to the underpasses. Or it could be a case of a "thought form" developing, much like the infamous "Phillip" experiment conducted by a psychical circle several years ago. They came up with the name Phillip, wrote a completely fake backstory for him and then began trying to contact the "spirit." Eventually, they did indeed establish contact with "Phillip," and he confirmed the details of his "life." It was never shown whether this was a thought form or a masquerading spirit, but "Lydia" could be the same thing, acting out the details of the legend. We know, it sounds farfetched to us too, but who knows?

There is one other possibility. We know no one wants to hear it, but Lydia could simply be an urban legend. The vanishing hitchhiker is a motif that is widespread across the United States, Canada and Europe. There is at least one such story in every state. North Carolina has at least five such stories, two of which take place in Michael's home county of Yadkin.

The names are different—Mary, Lydia, Lara, Allison, Christine, etc.—and the details vary, but the basic story of a girl picked up on the side of the road and then vanishing are the same. A lot of people think this means they are all "just stories."

Michael thinks a little differently, and Amy tentatively agrees. Michael's theory is that the very fact that there are so many stories indicates that this type of spirit or residual actually exists. After all, there are a very few where there are indeed actual records of real people who died in the manner described. Take note of Skip Westmoreland, who appears in the chapter "Three Little Indians and Other Tales." However, we see the point made by those who declare all such tales to be urban legends.

In any event, Lydia has not made a documented appearance in several years—decades, actually. Perhaps she has finally joined her loved ones on the far side of Jordan—or maybe she simply finally made it into the house.

This is another bone of contention—that address. In Michael's first book, he made the argument clear: anyone who picked up a girl who then vanished into thin air would have that address seared into their memory forever. How is it that, over the years, not one single person has let that address slip or come forward and said, "I own this house"?

Shortly thereafter, we began to see apologists coming up with theories that it was to "protect her family's privacy" or the owners after "Lydia's" family swore everyone to secrecy. Well, the first no longer holds water. The story

The second underpass. *Photo by Michael Renegar.*

says Lydia was an only child in most versions, and her parents would be long dead. They no longer need to be protected. And, as for the latter, as they say, if two people know something, it is a secret only if one of them is dead. *Someone* would have spilled the beans by now.

Amy is a sensitive, and she feels that something sad and tragic did indeed take place at the old underpass many years ago. And she believes there is some sort of presence out there, though whether it is the lonely girl is something we will always wonder about. Real or not, Lydia will always hold a special place in the hearts of those who love North Carolina and its ghostly legends.

Real Ghosts at Spookywoods?

On Kersey Valley Road in High Point, you can find one of the best and biggest haunted attractions in the United States. For more than a quarter of a century, Spookywoods has offered thrills and chills to thousands of children and adults alike. But lurking behind the scenes, there are *real* ghosts and spirits on the prowl.

In the early 1930s, according to Steven, an employee of Kersey Valley, Inc., a farming family lived in the old house. The Great Depression was on, and times were tough. The family took in boarders on occasion. One day, a traveler's car broke down on the road near the farmhouse. The kind farmer and his family took the fellow in. We aren't sure how long the stranger was with them. After supper, their guest would pull out his fiddle and play a few tunes for the family. The kids especially enjoyed listening to the lilting melodies "the fiddler" would play.

Unfortunately, their entertaining guest became ill. He was already quite large, and his body swelled to alarming proportions. Heart disease was the diagnosis. Soon, it became too difficult for the man to make his way down the narrow staircase. He began to take his meals in his bedroom upstairs.

One day, the lady of the house sent one of her children up to check on the poor man. The child came back down and told his mother something was wrong. He couldn't wake the big man. Already suspecting the worst, the woman went upstairs. Sure enough, she found the guest stone cold dead. He'd had a massive heart attack.

They removed his body through the upstairs window. *Photo by Amy Spease.*

The children were heartbroken. They'd loved the fiddler, and now they would never hear his music again. When the family called for help and tried to move his body, they discovered a real problem. The man was just too big and heavy for them to carry him down the stairs. After some discussion, they figured it out. They'd have to use a pulley and haul his poor body out the upstairs window. Carefully, the fiddler's body was hoisted out the window and lowered to the ground, where a hearse awaited. The fiddler's body was taken away, and the family settled down to its normal routine—almost.

Soon after the musical guest's death, the family began to hear strange things in the house. Footsteps sounded on the floor above even though no one was up there at the time. They were heavy, shuffling steps, much like their departed guest had made just prior to his demise. Then one night after supper, they heard something startling and unexpected; the strains of a fiddle floated down to them from the floor above. It was unquestionably one of the tunes the fiddler had played for them. The farmer and his oldest son rushed up the steps, but the music had stopped. There was no one there.

At first, it was a little frightening. But eventually, the family grew accustomed to the nightly display of ghostly fiddle playing. They were even comforted and touched that the friendly man had chosen to return to them and continue to entertain them with his music. If a visitor heard the strange noses and music, the farmer or one of them would say, "Oh, don't worry. That's just the fiddler playing us a tune." Many a visitor left scratching their heads at the strange occurrences. The house gained a reputation as a "hain't."

Flash-forward several decades. Tony, the new owner of the property, who used to camp there with his friends, opened up a spook trail on the property with a handful of people helping him. By 2011, Spookywoods had grown to include dozens of acres and employed more than three hundred people. It is the largest such haunted attraction in North Carolina, with thousands of visitors each year from all around the world. Few of these guests ever realize that *some* of the spooky things they see and hear just might be the real deal.

We knew Sarah Sherman and Michelle Kindley from their days with the Winston-Salem Paranormal Society (WSPS). They were part of that group when they joined our old group, Project Ghost-Find, in an overnight investigation of Sci-Works, a science educational museum in Winston-Salem built on the site of the old County Home, Hospital, Asylum and Sanatorium. They now have their own paranormal investigation team, Autumn Moon.

Jimmy Tomlin, a High Point newspaper reporter, told Michael about the alleged real ghosts at Spookywoods. He then called Tonya Denny of the WSPS to see if she knew anything about it. Tonya said that Sarah worked out there, so Michael contacted Sarah. She set up an interview with Steven Lee, who also works there and knew the story of the fiddler.

At the beginning of February 2011, Amy and Michael drove down to Kersey Valley to talk to Steven, Sarah and Michelle. They arrived around 4:00 p.m. Sarah met us at the gate by the old farmhouse, and we went inside and sat down on a sofa in the living room. The house is now a "spook house" and has a door rigged to slam with the wind. This proved disconcerting a couple of times. Relics of the spooky performances were everywhere, including some rather convincing bloody handprints on a wall.

Steve related the story of the fiddler to us, and we asked questions. He did not know the name of the family involved. Later, Michael would do some research, and Karen at the High Point Library Research Department took a look too. She found several families associated with the property and that it had once been divided up into several lots. The families she found associated with pieces of the property include the Ferries, the Ingrams, the Inmans, etc. The first sale she found was in 1918 and involved the Armstrong family selling a large tract to the Spainhours. We were never able to determine if any of these families were connected to the house, though the Frederick Spainhour family did indeed have a boarder, one Charlie Inman, who appears to have been a relative of Frederick's wife. Their address, however, was listed as Providence Road. This may have been what Kersey Valley was originally called, though we weren't able to determine that. Mr. Inman didn't die in the house, however. He passed away at St. Lee's Hospital from old age/senility and pneumonia. He was an invalid, having a broken leg, and had been unable to walk for quite some time. We feel it is possible this man is indeed the origin of the fiddler story, though the details of his death differ from the legend. Stories often get twisted, altered and embellished with the retelling.

Steve and the ladies told us about different workers at the theme park hearing someone walking around upstairs when no one was there and how some people were touched by an unseen presence. Sarah and Michelle told of an investigator named John who tried to verbally provoke a response from any spirit in the house. He felt a burning sensation and discovered several fresh scratch marks on his body.

While WSPS members were visiting as guests of Sarah and Michelle, they experienced several odd incidents. Sarah and Michelle described how, as someone asked for a sign of the spirit's presence, a tube of horror makeup came flying out of the upstairs room where the fiddler died and landed on the floor at their feet. Tonya, the WSPS leader, scratched her foot. As she looked at it, Sarah was recording with a digital recorder. When she played it back, there was a distinctly male voice telling them to "Get out!"

Steven did a lot of the building and rigging of "spooks" in the house. He would sometimes get a deep feeling of nausea and uneasiness in the house, especially when he was alone, and he felt a tightness in his chest. Others experienced this on different occasions. Were they getting a residual affect from the fiddler's heart attack?

There may also be a second male spirit in the house. Sarah said she always got a sense that someone was shot in the house, probably by someone else, but she wasn't sure. When we researched the property later, we found no evidence of a shooting, but that doesn't mean much. It could have happened years before records were taken, perhaps even in the days shortly after European explorers settled the New World.

In the living room, or "common room" as the workers call it, Sarah and Michelle recorded one of the clearest EVP ever captured in the compound.

As they sat there, Michelle saw a shadowy figure dart across the room. When Sarah and Michelle played back their recorders, they heard a male voce growl, "F—k you!" This was captured on both recorders. They had also captured what sounded like a different voice, whom they believe to be the fiddler, that said, "Leave me alone!" Another recording caught a singing spirit calling, "They're from the ghetto, like me…" Along with this, they heard the sound of a piano note sounding—even though there was no piano in the house, nor was there any radio/player at the time. The expletive doesn't sound in character with the fiddler, and thus they believe that is evidence of the second male ghost.

Sarah experienced a touch in the upstairs of the house. She was in the bedroom where the fiddler died and felt a whoosh of air, which was followed by the back of her head being yanked forcibly back by her hair. While they do not believe there is anything negative on the property, this pulling of hair and cursing trouble us. Ghosts can be pranksters sometimes, but they rarely cause anything harmful, like scratching or cursing those present or pulling their hair.

Sarah and Michelle started working at Spookywoods in 2006. They would meet every night before the trail opened and walk to their scene in the woods. As they walked one night, they heard a whistling behind them. It stopped when they turned around but resumed when they began moving again and followed them all the way to their place.

Steven also related an incident that happened to him as he was delivering food to a worker in the graveyard scene. As he was talking to an actress portraying a zombie, he looked up, and in the spotlight shining on the scene, he saw a dark shadow figure move diagonally away from him, from a fake mausoleum to the right and some trees and "graves." Whatever it was, it blocked out the tombstones, trees, lights and implements behind it as it moved. But there was no sound, and the figure was a foot or two above the ground. Steven said nothing but moved along.

Many workers have experienced things in the woods. Dark shadow figures have been seen moving around. Sometimes they will peer out from behind trees only to disappear when someone investigates. Some of them seem to be adult sized; others are small, like the forms of children. Sometimes, the voices of multiple children are heard, even though none are present on the compound when this happens. Native American tribes once roamed these lands, so perhaps these elusive shadow figures are echoes of the ancient past.

Evidence of Native American spirits has been discovered. Several EVP recordings have captured the drums, chanting and singing of American

Indians on the property, both in the woods and in the field, which, in the fall, holds the corn maze known as the Maize Adventure.

Deeper in the woods, Sarah thinks there might be a spectral farmer. Once, when Tonya asked out there if the spirit knew the girls' names, the recorder captured the reply, "Yulp!"

Heavy plastic hangs everywhere, separating the different areas (one of which is a replica of the Michael Myers house from the horror movie classic *Halloween*...yipes!). One evening they noticed a huge industrial fan spinning, though there was absolutely no breeze blowing and the thing was unplugged. They also saw something hit the plastic very hard and heard footsteps running away, even though they saw no one.

Strange balls of light of varying colors have been seen on the spook trail as well, especially in the "Dark Dungeon" of the castle. They bob and weave about. Sometimes one may be able to follow them until they vanish into thin air.

Amy felt the presence of the fiddler in the house quite clearly. He is a solitary fellow now and really would rather just be left alone. She also

The entrance to the Spookywoods haunted trail. *Photo by Amy Spease.*

noticed a more aggressive feeling. She felt this second presence was the one responsible for scratching people and the pulling of hair. She seems to feel this one could hurt somebody if people aren't careful. She felt chills running up her spine and her hair standing on end the whole time we were in the house.

Outside, Amy later told Michael she actually *saw* the spirit of a Native American brave standing in the trees. He seemed to be waiting or watching for someone. When he noticed that she had seen him, the Indian inclined his head and smiled slightly. Amy has Native American heritage, and so does Michael. What she saw was probably one of the many Indian spirits on the property. After all, this was *their* land long before anyone else laid claim to it.

The Spookywoods Haunted Attraction is open from late September to early November. Kersey Valley, Inc., also operates the Maize Adventure and Kersey Valley Christmas. They also have several miles of ziplines that crisscross the property. There is something for just about everyone at Kersey Valley. When you go, pay attention. It may be that not *all* the ghosts, ghouls and monsters you encounter are actors.

Kersey Valley, Inc.
1615 Kersey Valley Road; High Point, NC 27263
Info@Spookywoods.com; www.kerseyvalleyzipline.com

After October 1, tickets are available by phone at 336-285-0548.

Note: Further investigation revealed that Charlie Inman did not die until 1953, years after he lived with the Spainhours and fifteen years after they sold the property. While he may still be the inspiration for the legend, there may also have been another family with a boarder later on. Records are not available at this time to check. They become available in 2015.

HERSCHEL

Stephanie sighed as she stepped into the costume room. She needed a derby for a prop. Surely there was one in here. As she looked for a hat, she suddenly felt a rush of cold air on the back of her neck, as if someone had exhaled directly on her skin. The startled girl whirled around, but no one was there. Goosebumps popped up on her arms. Suddenly, the light went out. But Stephanie didn't run for the door. She knew what was happening.

"Herschel, doggone it!" she snapped. "Stop it! I don't have time for any nonsense!"

The chill faded, and the light came back on. There, on a nearby chair, sat a black derby. Stephanie smiled and shook her head. "Thanks, Herschel!" she called as she picked it up and exited the costume room. "Sorry I yelled at you!"

That was more than twenty years ago. Stephanie went on to graduate from High Point University, and she now teaches drama at another school in North Carolina. This wasn't her first encounter with Herschel, the playful spirit that once inhabited Memorial Auditorium at HPU, but it was her last.

For many years, all theater students at High Point University knew the sad story of the theater ghost. Herschel was said to be a student at the school in the 1950s. He was a theater major and wrote several plays. He decided to produce one of them.

Other students agreed to help by working the sets and acting the parts. But Herschel took it all just a little too seriously for everyone else. He declared that his play would be "the greatest tragedy of all time." The young man's fellow thespians began to find Herschel to be too full of himself. They laughed and made fun of him. But Herschel didn't find their teasing to be funny at all. He just couldn't take it. On opening night, he went into the costume room and hanged himself.

Shortly after Herschel's dramatic exit, students and faculty began to whisper that there was a ghost haunting Memorial Auditorium. Most people believed the resident phantom was none other than the unfortunate Herschel.

It was mostly small stuff that people would experience. Disembodied footsteps sounded in empty hallways. Window blinds would be disturbed when no one was near them. On rare occasions, the ghost might throw some object from the costume room across that room or the stage. He would turn lights on and off. A few times, Herschel did show himself as a fleeting shadow on the wall.

A very famous incident occurred in the 1990s. The theater troupe was performing the play *Oliver*, an adaptation of the Charles Dickens classic *Oliver Twist*. In the middle of the production, an alumnus decided to change seats. Seconds after the patron was settled in his new seat, a large stage lamp fell, crashing into the very seat he had just left. If he hadn't moved, the alumnus would probably have joined Herschel in his spectral activities. Some said that Herschel had somehow subliminally warned the man that he was in danger and needed to move. Others thought something more sinister had happened. They whispered that the man had been a classmate of Herschel's, one of the students who had tormented the poor young man. Herschel, recognizing him, had sought revenge.

This does not seem to fit with the normally benign activities of the ghost. Herschel usually just acts out harmless pranks. But who knows? If he did recognize the patron as one of the people who drove him to take his own life, perhaps he was seized by a fit of rage. If ghosts are the remnants of departed human beings, then they remain the same people as they were in life. If he thought that this man was responsible for his depression and death, one can see where Herschel might want a comeuppance, even if such an attack was wrong, even against his usual nature. Either way, the man was not harmed, so maybe Herschel realized it was wrong to harm him, or maybe the first set of people are right and Herschel simply saved someone's life. We think we prefer *that* explanation.

The ghost of the sad student continued to haunt Memorial Auditorium throughout its existence. Herschel played his tricks on generation after generation of students and staff. Across more than four decades, hundreds of people heard his tragic story, and dozens of them actually experienced his ghostly fun. And you know, perhaps he was right after all. The way he ended up, perhaps his play *was* the "greatest tragedy of all time," at least for him.

Herschel's antics became legend, and he wasn't forgotten. People at High Point University loved their ghost, and he returned the affection, touching them in the dark, playing with the lights and even showing himself to the rare person honored with such an appearance. Anyone who ever had a run-in with Herschel will tell you that he was very, very real.

Memorial Auditorium at High Point University was demolished in August 2005 to make room for more modern buildings. The familiar stage, costume room and hallways Herschel knew are gone forever. We haven't heard whether Herschel has taken up residence in the new digs. But if you go to High Point University and encounter a brief chill, hear footsteps when no one is there or experience a touch on your arm by an unseen hand, don't be frightened. Just say, "Is that you, Herschel?" and introduce yourself. You might just make a new friend and help perpetuate the memory of the poor playmaker, Herschel.

J.H. ADAMS INN

Across the South, many stately old homes have been transformed, in recent years, into restaurants, inns or bed-and-breakfast establishments. This trend has helped to save many historic homes and businesses from the wrecking ball and allows many people to enjoy a taste of the past they might not get to experience otherwise.

The early twentieth century was a busy time in the Triad. R.J. Reynolds was building his tobacco empire in Winston-Salem; Moses Cone, the "Denim King," was producing textiles at his mills in Greensboro; and numerous other local businessmen were building their businesses. John Hampton Adams was one of these rising industrialists.

John "Hamp" Adams was born in 1885 in Marlboro County, South Carolina. He moved to High Point and became associated with James Henry Millis, a well-known businessman. Adams soon was Millis's apprentice and convinced the businessman to go into the hosiery business. They started the High Point Hosiery Mill, which produced two hundred pairs of black stockings every day. By 1927, they had consolidated several hosiery mills in High Point into one company, the Adams-Millis Corporation. In 1928, this company was listed with the New York Stock Exchange. For many decades, Adams-Millis was one of only a handful of North Carolina companies listed on the "Big Board."

J.H. Adams was known as a quiet man with a lot of energy, a keen business senses and a persevering determination at anything he did. He was a director of Wachovia Bank & Trust, an investor in the local paper, a

J.H. Adams Inn. *Photo by Michael Renegar.*

mason, a trustee of the Oak Ridge Institute and one of the founders of the High Point Country Club.

The original Adams home was on English Road across from the main mill. A beautiful mansion was started at 1108 North Main Street in High Point in 1917 and was completed the following year. This lovely home would be the private residence for J.H. Adams and his family, which included his wife, Elizabeth Barnes Adams (they were married in 1906), and two daughters, Elizabeth and Nell. They lived there for nearly twenty years. Elizabeth Barnes Adams was a widely popular and active lady in High Point society. For her entire life, she was active in the community, and echoes of her influence remain even today.

The house was constructed in the Italian Renaissance style. It is a soft pastel color, a light pinkish brown in appearance, at least in photographs. It was filled with the grand décor and furniture of the period. The family was quite comfortable in the spacious home. They entertained guests and business associates of Adams and Millis, as well as hosted society functions.

In 1930, Adams and his family moved to a new home in Sedgefield. Hamp passed away on January 31, 1935. Four years later, Adams's daughters and their families donated the manse at 1108 North Main to the High Point YWCA. The YWCA occupied the J.H. Adams House until about 1960, when the property was taken over by the Harold C. Davis Funeral Home, Chapel of Flowers. In May 2011, Michael spoke with Mr. Leigh Davis, who still operates the Davis Funeral Service at its new location on Phillips Avenue in High Point.

Mr. Davis told Michael that the Chapel of Flowers operated at the Adams House from 1960 until 1996. When asked if he or any of his staff had ever experienced anything of a paranormal nature while at the Adams House, Mr. Davis replied in the negative. To his knowledge, nothing like that occurred during the Chapel of Flowers' tenure at the stately mansion.

One story that has been told over the years is that a young woman died at the funeral home after an automobile accident nearby. Not too many years ago, ambulance services, especially in small towns or rural areas, were run by the funeral homes. This young lady was allegedly taken to the Adams House, where she was said to have died.

This story really didn't make sense to us. Why would a *living* person be taken to a funeral home instead of the hospital? Mr. Davis said that no such incident ever occurred to his knowledge. In fact, he said that he didn't know of anyone dying in the house during the time his family's funeral service was there. He did, however, recall that he had heard that a member of the Adams family's service staff died on the property back when the Adamses themselves were still in residence. He did not know the circumstances of this death or the time period in which it occurred. If the person were on the Adams staff, it would have had to have been between 1918 and 1930, if it happened while the family was living there.

So who was this staff member who passed away? Was it a man or a woman? Does the unfortunate staffer's ghost remain in the J.H. Adams House?

In early 2000, extensive renovations and restorations began on the old mansion. In the fall of 2001, the grand old dame opened up as the J.H. Adams Inn. The inn offers more than thirty unique rooms and suites with luxurious accommodations and furnishings. No two rooms are exactly alike. The inn offers high-speed Internet access, wake-up calls, a fitness room and rooms for meetings. Guests receive a continental breakfast, a complimentary glass of wine and a warm, welcoming atmosphere. Hampton's is the in-house restaurant and offers a wide variety of dining services. And, for those interested, you may also receive a visit from a ghostly occupant.

The ghost of none other than John Hampton Adams himself is said to roam his former home. His apparition has been seen in the room that was his private accommodations in the '20s and '30s. He always seems to be smoking a cigar, one of his favorite vices. The smell of a cigar is said to permeate the room when his ghost is present. One guest saw a ghostly figure in that room. Later, when she saw a photograph of Adams in the bar, she identified him as the man she had seen. Staff members have seen the businessman in other areas of the house as well, including the kitchen. One staff member is said to have seen him walk directly through a wall.

Some people have apparently refused to eat in the front parlor, remembering that this is where they'd attended the funeral of a loved one or friend. Some also appeared skeptical of the idea of staying in an inn once used as a funeral home. This apparently led some to deny the presence of ghosts in the inn.

Bo Blackburn is a friend of ours. He runs a ghost investigation team dubbed Mystery Inc., in honor of the "Scooby Gang" from the popular cartoon series and major motion pictures featuring the clumsy and loveable Great Dane Scooby Doo. He was contacted by Mena, the hotel manager, and took his team to the inn to check out the stories of ghostly activity in February 2010.

Bo had three team members with him for this first investigation: his wife, Johneka (known as Jay); tech specialist Raymond H.; and spirit sensitive Tiffany C. When they arrived at the inn, Bo conferred with the manager, and the team set up its base of operations in what had been J.H. Adams's personal room when he resided there.

As they made their way to the room, Tiffany was immediately drawn to a door that was just to the right of the base room. This door turned out to lead to the attic. Bo had previously been told that employees did not like to go up there at all. When they had to, they did whatever they had to do as quickly as possible and got out of there. Bo doesn't provide details about a case to his team members beforehand and was pleased that his sensitive had correctly zoomed in on one of the places deemed active.

The team set up their base computer and other equipment, and then Ray began a photographic sweep of all the available rooms. An HD camera was set up in the base room in hopes of caching J.H. Adams up to his ghostly tricks. While Bo and Jay got baseline EMF and temperature readings in J.H.'s main room, Ray and Tiffany went across the hall into a room where the ghost had been seen before as well.

In an interview, Bo had talked to a man and his daughter who had actually lived in the hotel. The young woman had been awakened one night in that room by a bald man. At first, she'd thought the man was her father, but she realized he was a stranger when her eyes became more accustomed to the darkness. The man turned and walked away, vanishing. This is the young woman who identified J.H. Adams from the photograph.

After about an hour, Bo sent Jay to join Tiffany and had Ray come into the Adams room with him. Tiffany and Jay found an anomaly in the readings on their equipment and followed the anomaly down the stairs into a bathroom. One person had reported seeing the apparition of Adams walk into this bathroom and disappear.

Bo and Jay remained downstairs while sending Tiffany and Ray to the attic. They stayed in the attic for about half an hour. When they returned to the base room, both reported seeing some weird shadow movement up there. So Bo and Jay went up to the dark attic, where he began taking EMF readings while she took photos.

Once his eyes became accustomed to the spare lighting, Bo noticed that light was indeed coming in the attic windows. There was a streetlight about a block away, and when it would change, the lighting and shadows in the attic subtly changed as well. He felt this was probably the reason they saw the shadows "moving." Tiffany, however, insisted that she sensed several spirits present.

Bo, however, was unconvinced. Only later, upon review of the material, did he decide that there was indeed something going on in the attic. In two separate photos, a misty-looking string of apparent light was visible. People often call these strings of light vortexes, though they often turn out to be merely camera straps. Bo thinks these are genuine vortexes, however. One of the photos is included here for the readers to make up their own minds.

There was also an interesting audio anomaly. Tiffany had been conducting an EVP session in the attic. On playback, a voice calls out, "Tiffany, help me!" Was there some sort of doorway up there through which the entities Tiffany reported were coming in and out of the inn?

Bo next sent Ray and Tiffany to the basement fitness room. He did not tell them what this room had once been. In fact, it is where bodies were stored when the building was a funeral home, according to staff. The two came back up after only a few minutes. Tiffany was quite upset and said the room felt "full of the dead." She thought hundreds of people had died there and wanted to know just what had gone on in that room. Realizing he had to calm his team down, Bo explained to them that the building had been a funeral home and that that particular room had held the bodies awaiting preparation and such. To his knowledge, no one had died in there. Bo went into the room—which he called a morgue in his report—with Ray. The other man told him almost immediately that the room felt much lighter than it had when he was in there with Tiffany. Bo speculates that since Tiffany is sensitive, the spirits might have been pressing more in on her, attempting to make contact. Spirits do indeed seem to actively be more attracted to people who have developed their psychic sensitivity. At this time, Bo conducted an EVP session in the fitness room. When he played the recording back, close to the beginning, there was a very loud cry of "Help me!" This suggests that perhaps at least one spirit may feel trapped in the location.

There is another rumor concerning the property. Bo was told by one staffer that someone was buried on the property when it was the Chapel of Flowers. This seems highly unlikely, as this was the last half of the twentieth century, with the Davis family operating its services there from 1960 to 1996. Bo turned up no evidence that there was any truth to this story. Bo went back to the J.H. Adams Inn to share his evidence. He talked to the manager and some of the staff. He told them that the consensus of his people was that the inn was indeed haunted. He even suggested they might want to have a cleansing of the place done in order to free any spirits that might be trapped there.

Is this a vortex (an opening to some other dimension)? *Photo by Bo Blackburn.*

Is John Hampton Adams still coming back to the home he loved so much? Does he stay there, or does he simply pop in periodically to check on things? Is he pleased with the current status of his home as an inn? And are there other ghosts present? Who was this staff member who served the Adams family? Did this person really die on the property, and if so, is the staffer's spirit still somehow connected to the place? Are there spirits connected to its years as a place of mourning? And what about the YWCA? Were there any deaths on the property during its twenty-odd years under that capacity?

The answers to these questions are likely out there and may be found by some future researcher or historian. In the meantime, if you choose to stay at the J.H. Adams Inn, keep an eye out. Not all of your fellow guests may be of flesh and bone.

The J.H. Adams Inn
1108 North Main Street; High Point, NC 27262
336-882-3267 or 1-888-256-1289; info@jhadamsinn.com

Note: We identified one servant of the Adamses, Mr. John Irvin, who died while in their service. He had served as chauffer, as well as a butler. However, he died in 1938 while employed by Mrs. Adams at the Sedgefield Mansion. If another servant passed away at the High Point residence, he or she has not been identified.

IN CONCLUSION

So, there you have it—a brief tour of just some of the places in the Triad where ghosts allegedly roam. We hope you have enjoyed these stories and that maybe, just maybe, you might have learned a little bit of the history of the Triad as well. You have read about several famous local haunts and also about some that have never before been published. We have tried to be as true to the original legends as possible but also to give you the facts about the cases. Do ghosts really exist? Well, *we* believe so. We have found no evidence to prove they do not exist and vast amounts of evidence and personal experiences to support that they do. In the end, you must be your own judge on their account. No one can prove ghosts exist to a confirmed skeptic, nor can anyone disprove them to a confirmed believer. So be safe, and happy hauntings!

Selected Bibliography

Calloway, Burt, and Jennifer FitzSimmons. *Triad Hauntings*. Winston-Salem, NC: Bandit Books, 1990.

Casstevens, Frances H. *Ghosts of the North Carolina Piedmont*. Charleston, SC: The History Press, 2009.

Renegar, Michael. *Roadside Revenants and Other North Carolina Ghosts and Legends*. Fairview, NC: Bright Mountain Books, 2005.

———. *Tar Heel Terrors: More North Carolina Ghosts and Legends*. Fairview, NC: Bright Mountain Books, 2011.

Roberts, Nancy. *North Carolina Ghosts and Legends*, Columbia: University of South Carolina Press, 1991.

Photo by Rocky Spease.

About the Authors

Michael Renegar was raised in East Bend, North Carolina, where he still resides. He is an avid guitarist, songwriter and student of history. Sherry Holley, niece of rock 'n' roll founding father Buddy Holly, has recorded some of his music. Michael grew up listening to relatives and friends tell ghost stories and has set out to record as many of these old legends as possible. He attended Appalachian State University in Boone, North Carolina, and founded a loose group of ghost hunters that checked out campus legends and tales from around the region.

Michael is a model photographer and the co-founder of Camel City Spirit Seekers, a ghost investigative group based in Winston-Salem, North Carolina. He is the author of two previous collections of North Carolina ghost stories.

Amy Spease is a native of Winston-Salem. She still lives there with her husband, David, and two children, Rocky and Jade. She is an eclectic soul and collects many things, from odd antiques to 1950s tableware. Amy is part American Indian and embraces that heritage. She is an artist and has also been an alternative model since 2005. Her love of ghosts and the paranormal has been a huge part of her life since childhood, and she adores her home state and its rich history and ghostlore. Writing and being an author were childhood dreams of hers. This is her first published book. She is the co-founder of Camel City Spirit Seekers.

Michael and Amy met in 2006 as a result of his photography and her modeling. They have become great friends and treat each other as brother and sister. They have been working together on photo projects and ghost hunting ever since. The group they founded has been investigating ghostly legends and recording them since 2008. They hope to author several more collections of these haunting stories, for their enjoyment as well as yours.

Visit us at
www.historypress.net